"Mike McKinley has done it again. _____
previous book, *The Cross in your Life* (formerly titled *Passion*),
Mike focuses on the resurrection of Jesus in a way that is
theologically precise, pastorally driven, and practically helpful.
The Resurrection In Your Life is this faithful, winsome pastor at
his best, holding up the prism of the resurrection and showing
its biblical layers of beauty and wonder as he turns it for the
reader to see. This book is accessible for everyone, written both
to capture unbelievers and feed the soul of the discouraged
saint who has lost sight of that unshakable hope Jesus secured
for those in him. I heartily commend this book and its author."

*Brian Croft, Senior Pastor, Auburndale Baptist Church, Kentucky;
Founder of Practical Shepherding*

"The wonder of Christ's resurrection is put on glorious display
in this book. We are taken through the promises of God kept,
shown and amplified in the resurrection of Jesus Christ. Mike
charts the unfurling beauty of the resurrection through the
writings of Luke, leading to deep theological reflection on the
significance of Jesus rising, ascending and ruling, and on the
coming of the Spirit at Pentecost. At the same time, he keeps
the doctrine rooted in Jesus himself. The result is a book that is
simple and striking, surprising us as it shows us Jesus. I plan on
recommending this book widely."

*John Hindley, Pastor of BroadGrace, Norfolk; author of "Serving
Without Sinking" and "You Can Really Grow"*

"Mike McKinley has now written a worthy sequel to *The Cross in
Your Life*. It is a rich feast of prose, both in style and substance.
The cross and the resurrection of Jesus Christ stand as two
powerful truths which form the very heart of Christianity. And
McKinley's excellent literary capturing of these two profound
realities are a joy to read and reflect upon. It will show how
the resurrection applies to your most fundamental needs in
life, death and beyond. And it will cause you to bow down and
worship the One who died and rose again on your behalf."

Lance Quinn, Pastor, Thousand Oaks Bible Church, California

"Mike McKinley has once again provided a sparkling exposition on a key moment in the life of Jesus and the history of the world. Too often the resurrection is neglected as a mere appendix to the cross, but Mike shows its everyday relevance with clarity, wit and wonderful encouragement. This is highly recommended."

Sam Allberry, Associate Pastor of St Mary's Maidenhead; author of "Is God Anti-Gay?" and "Lifted: Experiencing the Resurrection Life"

MIKE McKINLEY

THE
RESURRECTION
IN YOUR LIFE

How the living Christ
changes your world

About the author

Mike McKinley is Pastor of Sterling Baptist Church in Sterling, Virginia. He is married to Karen, and they have five children. Mike received his MDiv from Westminster Theological Seminary, Philadelphia, and is author of *The Cross In Your Life* (formerly titled *Passion*), *Did The Devil Make Me Do It?* and *Am I Really A Christian?*

For my Mom,
whose life and love
is a picture of God's grace.

The Resurrection In Your Life:
How the Living Christ Changes Your World
© Michael McKinley/The Good Book Company, 2015.

Published by

The Good Book Company
Tel (UK): 0333 123 0880;
International: +44 (0) 208 942 0880
Email: admin@thegoodbook.co.uk

Websites:

N America: www.thegoodbook.com
UK: www.thegoodbook.co.uk
Australia: www.thegoodbook.com.au
New Zealand: www.thegoodbook.co.nz

ISBN: 9781910307038

Printed and bound by CPI Group (UK) Ltd, Croydon, CR0 4YY
Design by André Parker

CONTENTS

THE STORY DOESN'T STOP

I love stories. Some of my favorite childhood memories are set in my hometown's local library, where I would load up on books to devour on long summer days. (Yes, I was a major nerd, thanks for asking.)

Now that I have five kids of my own, I spend far more time reading stories to them than I do working through the stacks of novels on my bedside table. And whether it is reading *Cinderella* to my preschool set or *Around the World in 80 Days* to my older kids, most great stories seem to follow the same basic outline. First, there's an introduction to the main character and his or her world (meet Cinderella). Next up comes the main character's problem (Cinderella's family is unkind to her), and then a potential solution that holds the promise of happiness (a fairy godmother and a good-looking prince!) But then, just when you think things are going to end well, there's a crisis that calls everything into question (the stroke of midnight!) Only at the end do we get the final resolution that makes sense of the crisis and assures the happiness of the main character (a duke with a glass slipper and a whole bunch of happily ever after!)

Now, imagine how badly it would mess up kids if we stopped reading all of their favorite stories before the end;

if we left Cinderella an unmarried maid, forever looking back on her one night at the ball. Or if we left Harry Potter dead on the floor after Voldemort's curse. Of course, sooner or later they'll come across books without a happy ending—those adult novels where the ending is sad, clever, and leaves us desperate inside because there's something in us that demands a happy ending in a book, even if we've learned not always to expect it in life. The most satisfying stories finish on a note of hope, with at least a hint of happiness.

Well, the story of the Bible is most certainly not a fairy tale. But with God as its author, it has all of the hallmarks of a great story. At the beginning we are introduced to the main character of God's creation (humanity) and a serious problem (sin, rebellion and death). There's a promising solution to the problem (God's sent his very own Son), but then a terrible crisis that seems to undo everything (mankind crucified him!). It is only at that point that we see the final resolution that shows us the meaning of the cross and assures us that the story ends well for humanity: the resurrection and ascension of Jesus.

For Christians, the story that makes sense of our lives doesn't end with a suffering, crucified Savior. The cross is vitally important to our faith, but only because Jesus rose from the grave and ascended into heaven for us.

The resurrection matters. You know that already if you are a Christian; but do you know *why* it matters? Often, we can end up treating the resurrection as though it were God's way of tying up the loose ends; the cross is where everything important happens, but then there's a dead body that needs dealing with. Or we can be so busy trying to prove the resurrection really happened that we forget to be excited *that* it happened.

Of course, the cross is wonderful and foundational for our lives and human history. It's why I wrote the book that this is the sequel for, *The Cross In Your Life* (or, as it was originally titled, *Passion*), about the events of the last 24 hours of Jesus' earthly life; and (more importantly) it's why we'll spend eternity praising Jesus, the Lamb who was slain.

But the great thing is... there's more. The story doesn't stop at the wooden cross. It doesn't stop at the empty tomb. In fact, what's really amazing about this story is that it doesn't end, and will never end. When I come to the end of a great novel, I am sad that I have to leave it behind. The characters I had come to love and the world that I had entered into is all gone (until the sequel!) But the story of Jesus doesn't end. In many ways, it begins where it seemed to have ended—at his grave. The risen Jesus ascended into heaven and poured out his Spirit on his people so that we can live our lives in his resurrection power. At this moment, the joy and power of the resurrection, and its implications and impact are still being felt round the world, in millions of lives. It's a story with a page being written right now; every Christian finds himself or herself in the middle of the greatest story ever, the story of God's plan to save a people for his own glory. It's a story that has no final chapter, that extends into eternity with God, because the great ending (death) gets its teeth kicked in on page one.

This book is fundamentally about God's great What Happened Next; about his eternal Happy Ending. It is about the greatest story ever told, the story that is true, and the story that is (or could be) yours. If you are considering Christianity, I hope you'll see how your life needs to become part of this great narrative. And if you are a Christian—whether you have been following the Risen Jesus for days or for decades—my prayer is that your hearts will be captivated by the story of what the Risen Jesus has done, is doing and will do, and that your life will be lived out in light of it.

CHAPTER ONE

HE IS NOT HERE

I
⁵⁴ It was Preparation Day, and the Sabbath was about to begin.

⁵⁵ The women who had come with Jesus from Galilee followed Joseph and saw the tomb and how his body was laid in it. ⁵⁶ Then they went home and prepared spices and perfumes. But they rested on the Sabbath in obedience to the commandment.

¹ On the first day of the week, very early in the morning, the women took the spices they had prepared and went to the tomb. ² They found the stone rolled away from the tomb, ³ but when they entered, they did not find the body of the Lord Jesus. ⁴ While they were wondering about this, suddenly two men in clothes that gleamed like lightning stood beside them. ⁵ In their fright the women bowed down with their faces to the ground, but the men said to them, "Why do you look for the living among the dead? ⁶ He is not here; he has risen! Remember how he told you, while he was still with you in Galilee: ⁷ 'The Son of Man must be delivered over to the hands of sinners, be crucified and on the third day be raised again.'" ⁸ Then they remembered his words.

⁹ When they came back from the tomb, they told all these things to the Eleven and to all the others. ¹⁰ It was Mary Magdalene, Joanna, Mary the mother of James, and the others with them who told this to the apostles. ¹¹ But they did not believe the women, because their words seemed to them like nonsense. ¹² Peter, however, got up and ran to the tomb. Bending over, he saw the strips of linen lying by themselves, and he went away, wondering to himself what had happened.

Luke 23 v 54 – 24 v 12

There are few things that hurt more than your greatest hopes being utterly dashed. It is tough to top the misery of having all of your dreams come crashing down around you. When this kind of disappointment comes, it turns everything upside down—your past, your present and your future. *How could I have put my hope in something that wasn't true? This hurts so much, I can't think without it being right at the forefront of those thoughts. All the things I've been looking forward to will never, ever happen.*

If you have ever had your heart broken by someone you loved, or had a hero of yours prove to be a fraud, you know the feeling I'm talking about. It's like being punched in the stomach; it almost literally takes your breath away.

I wonder if that's how Jesus' followers were feeling on Friday evening after his crucifixion. We are diving into the Gospel of Luke almost at its end, with only just over a chapter to go. And to Jesus' friends, it was the end. Jesus' lifeless body had been wrapped in a shroud and placed in a tomb. Imagine the intense sense of loss that Mary Magdalene and Joanna and the other women must have been feeling. They would never see Jesus again. They would never again share in the joy of Jesus' friendship, his wise advice, or the loving care they had come to treasure from him. All they were left with was the vivid memory of his humiliation, his suffering, and his defeat at the hands of his enemies.

Perhaps worst of all, every hope that had grown up in their souls over the previous three years was now completely dashed. They had thought of Jesus as more than just a wise teacher and close friend; they had called him "Lord" and looked forward to the day when he would take his place as ruler over the nation of Israel. To lose a close friend would have been bad enough; but they had lost all their hopes, too. There would be no coming kingdom of God. There would be no glorious restoration of God's people. All they had left to do was to rest on the Sabbath (Friday night into Saturday), and then finish caring for their dead friend's body on the Sunday. A week before, all had been hope. Now, all was grief.

When we think about the events of the first Easter, it's easy to rush to the Sunday morning. But pause, and wait, and think. Take time to come alongside these grieving women—because it's only when you get inside the dashed hopes of these ladies that you are prepared to begin to appreciate what happens next.

He is Not Here

When the women arrived at the tomb early on that Sunday morning, they found three things that they were not expecting. First, the stone had been rolled away from the entrance to the grave. In those days, tombs were covered by a heavy stone; it would have required two fairly strong people to budge it. It must have been a relief when they walked up to the grave and saw that the stone was already moved for them.

The second surprise the women encountered was that the body of the Lord Jesus was no longer there. You can understand why that would have been startling for them; dead bodies don't run out to the corner store for a pint of ice cream. Their thoughts must have run wild: was this the work of vandals? Was this some kind of sick joke? Hadn't these past two days been heartbreaking enough? And now this! Relief must have turned to despair.

Then came the third shock to their system. Two men were standing beside the tomb in dazzling apparel. Luke does not tell us who they were, but it seems a pretty safe bet that these were angels from the Lord. A very high percentage of people in the Bible who show up in bright, shining clothing turn out to be angels—and the Gospels of Matthew and John spell out that these dazzling figures were indeed heavenly messengers.

These angels ask a very strange question: "Why do you look for the living among the dead?" The answer seems pretty obvious: the women are not looking for the living! The last time they saw Jesus, he was dead. Their last glimpse of him was him being laid in his tomb. Everything in their experience of death taught them that this was a terminal condition—the only One who had seemed to be able to overpower death had now succumbed to it. And so they knew that Jesus would be "among the dead." Of course they did!

But in fact, they were completely, wonderfully wrong. "He is not here; he has risen." Jesus is not dead; he is alive. He should be spoken of in the present tense, not the past.

He has risen. Three words that can wipe away all the loss and grief of the past days. Three words that change everything. He has risen. Minutes before, the women had known he was dead. But they were utterly mistaken. He has risen.

The Wonder of Being Wrong

Normally we don't enjoy being proven wrong. I know that I sometimes go to great lengths to avoid having to admit that I was in error about something. But for these women, being wrong was the best thing in the world! These women thought the death of Christ was the end; it was proof that he could not save them; it was the burial not only of their friend, but their hopes. And they were totally and gloriously wrong! The resurrection turns everything we know on its head. Death leads to life, weakness and suffering give way to glory, crushed dreams give way to living hope.

In a sense, becoming a Christian means being given eyes to see that you have been wrong. Whereas previously Jesus just seemed like some guy—a great teacher, a moral instructor, an irrelevant ancient martyr—now you can see that you were as wrong as you could be. Now you see that he is the living Lord, the one who gives life and peace and rest to all those who will come to him by faith. It's a wonderful thing when you realize that you've been wrong in that way!

Lots of great stories have some big revelation that makes you rethink everything that you thought was true before. In *Star Wars*, Darth Vader is Luke Skywalker's father (and Princess Leia's as well). Bruce Willis' character in *The Sixth Sense* is really (spoiler alert) dead. A fair way through *The Hunger Games*, we discover that Katniss Everdeen is really a pawn in a much larger rebellion against the Capital. When you have those pieces of information in place, you see the entire world of the film or novel differently. You realize that you have been misunderstanding much of the story up until that point. All that you thought you knew is now up for grabs.

The resurrection of Jesus is that moment in human history. It's the reality that flips everything on its head. Before you have eyes to see the risen Jesus, death is the end of everything. But once you can see him in that way, death becomes the entrance point to eternal life. Think about it for a second: one of the most self-evident and painful facts of human existence—that death is the end—turns out to be gloriously wrong. In fact, death is the door at which the

Christian leaves behind sin and suffering and weakness, and enters into eternal life in the presence of Jesus.

This is why Peter can say that Christians suffer trials "for a little while" (1 Peter 1 v 6), even when there was no hope that the persecution his readers were experiencing would come to an end in this life. This life is not, as previously suspected, all there is—in the great span of eternity, it is only "a little while"! This is why the author of Hebrews can say that Christians have been set free from the fear of death (Hebrews 2 v 15). Death is not, as it always seemed, the end; it is the end of the beginning, and the beginning of eternity. The resurrection of Jesus changes the way we think about everything. He has risen. Everything is up for grabs.

As He Told You

It's hard for us to imagine the surprise that the women felt when they discovered the empty tomb. We are familiar with the story; there is enough residual Christian memory in western culture that most people on the street know that Jesus was crucified and rose from the dead. But these women didn't have a lifetime of Easter baskets and eggs creating space in their brains for the resurrection. When they showed up at the garden, they were fully expecting to find Jesus still in the grave.

And yet, perhaps they shouldn't have been so surprised. The angels that greeted the women told them that they should have expected Jesus not to be among the dead. Why? Because Jesus had explained it already: "Remember how he told you, while he was still with you in Galilee: 'The Son of Man must be delivered over to the hands of sinners, be crucified and on the third day be raised again'" (Luke 24 v 6-7).

So while we can sympathize with the women's confusion, the angel reminds them that Jesus had told them to expect this. Specifically, Jesus had told his followers that after he was betrayed and crucified, he would be raised again on the third day. If you look at just two examples from the Gospel of Luke, you can see what the angels were talking about:

○ "And he said, 'The Son of Man must suffer many things and be rejected by the elders, the chief priests and the teachers of the law, and he must be killed and on the third day be raised to life.'" (Luke 9 v 22)

○ "Jesus took the Twelve aside and told them, 'We are going up to Jerusalem, and everything that is written by the prophets about the Son of Man will be fulfilled. He will be handed over to the Gentiles. They will mock him, insult him and spit on him; they will flog him and kill him. On the third day he will rise again.'" (Luke 18 v 31-33)

These women had followed Jesus to Jerusalem. They had seen him angrily rejected by the religious elites; had seen him handed over to the Roman governor to hear his death sentence; had watched the mockery, rage and spittle rain down on him; had seen the whip lash his back; had seen him killed. As Jews, they counted part days as a day—so the Sunday was the third day.

And they had forgotten the one thing that had not yet happened: "He will rise again."

Now, corrected by the angels, they have their "Aha" moment: "They remembered his words" (24 v 8). You can imagine all of the pieces falling into place like the tumblers in a combination lock that spring the whole device open when they come together. Now everything makes sense.

But not to everyone. The women return to the other disciples, explaining to the men what the angels had explained to them. You can imagine how excited the women were to tell everyone the good news that would turn their sadness into celebration! But the whole scene falls flat: "Their words seemed to them like nonsense" (v 11). The men thought the women were crazy. Their hearts were locked shut.

How could the disciples be so dense? Even if they didn't anticipate the resurrection, they certainly should have been able to see the connection between the teachings of Jesus and the reports of the women coming back from the burial site. But instead of putting the pieces together, the apostles thought their story was "nonsense." Only Peter (and John, the Gospel of John adds) bothered to go to the tomb to see for himself; he saw the evidence, and yet, where the women had left announcing the resurrection, Peter "went away, wondering to himself what had happened."

You and I are in a different position than the people in Luke's narrative. We stand on the far side of the cross and resurrection. It's much easier for us to step back and see how those events fit in with the bigger picture of Jesus' life and teaching. We can see how the ending of the story makes sense of all the parts that came before it.

But my guess is that there are times and situations in your life where you can understand a little bit of what the apostles and the women were feeling. The pain of the crucifixion caused them to forget and ignore the promises of the resurrection. And perhaps you have felt such loss and pain that it seemed, or still seems, impossible to remember and believe God's promises. Maybe there are seasons in your life when it feels like God's plan has gone awry and that any talk of hope seems like nonsense to you. Maybe you are very aware of the reality of death; you stare at it, but you can't stare through it.

In those times, remember the resurrection of the Lord Jesus. He has risen. Remember that trials and problems do not take God by surprise. The darkness of midnight does not mean that dawn is never coming; in fact, the longer we've been in the darkness, the closer we are to the dawn. Jesus kept his word to his followers; he suffered, and then he rose. If he was able to keep that promise, you can be sure that he will keep all of his promises to you.

So when you lose your job or illness comes, remember the promise that God makes in his word: "God will meet all your needs according to the riches of his glory in Christ Jesus" (Philippians 4 v 19).

And when the dark cloud of depression won't lift, remember that when we bring our troubles to God in prayer, he promises that "the peace of God, which transcends all understanding, will guard your hearts and your minds in Christ Jesus" (Philippians 4 v 7).

And when sin and temptation are clinging closely, remember that God promises that they will not overwhelm you: "God is faithful; he will not let you be tempted beyond what you can bear. But when you are tempted, he will also provide a way out so that you can endure it" (1 Corinthians 10 v 13).

And when the desires of your heart seem out of reach, remember the words that God spoke to Paul when the apostle pleaded for relief from the "thorn in my flesh" (2 Corinthians 12 v 7): "My grace is sufficient for you, for my power is made perfect in weakness" (v 9).

You can trust Jesus. He has risen. If he kept a promise to rise from the dead, you can be sure that he will keep every other promise as well.

If you are a Christian, there are likely times in your own life when, now you look back, you can see God bringing you through, even though at the time you wondered where he was. And if you are a Christian, then you can always look back to the moment that changed your whole life, when some hopeless women discovered an empty tomb. The angel's gentle rebuke to the women speaks to us in situations when hope seems gone and the future looks bleak: "Remember how he told you..." Look at your own life, but ultimately look back at the empty tomb. Jesus always keeps his promises.

A Living Savior

In the rest of this book, we are going to flesh out some of the wonderful ways that the reality of Jesus' resurrection changes the way we live. But for now, just stop and realize that the fact that Jesus rose from the dead means that he is the only one who can save us. A couple months after this Sunday morning, the apostle Peter—whose wondering had by then turned to rock-solid conviction—told the elites who had killed Jesus that God had raised him from the dead and then concluded:

> Salvation is found in no one else, for there is no other name under
> heaven given to mankind by which we must be saved. (Acts 4 v 12)

The resurrection is proof that Jesus is able save us. If Jesus were still in his tomb, he'd merely be the pitiable victim of state-sponsored violence and religious intolerance, a tragic lesson in the cruelty of the world. But that's not Jesus, because he is not dead. In the movies, the filmmakers demonstrate the incredible power of a certain character by showing that person surviving an overwhelming assault. So, for example, Iron Man gets hit with a nuclear warhead and then a 70-storey-high building collapses on him. And you know that Iron Man is a hard, hard man when he emerges triumphantly out of the smoking rubble. The evil guys took their best shot and couldn't defeat him; and because they failed to defeat him, they are now in a lot of trouble.

Well, the resurrection of Jesus is that same idea, only true! Death and sin and the devil took their best shot; they did their worst; they killed the Son of God. But Jesus wasn't defeated. He has risen. Death, the great implacable enemy of all humanity, which reduces all our achievements and accumulations to dust, has been crushed.

And so where else are you going to find a Savior like this? We live in a world with a million false saviors. There are countless religions to follow. And there are so many secular saviors, too: our careers, our bank accounts, our children, our sex lives—all promise hope and meaning. All of those things offer us a kind of salvation, the illusion of lasting purpose and meaning and joy. But they never deliver; they always leave us empty and wanting more. Life will conspire to take its best shot at all of those would-be saviors: the economy collapses and you lose the dream job; a loved one lets you down; false rumors ruin your reputation. None of those things are bullet-proof. The fact is, you can only be completely saved by one person, the indestructible risen Lord Jesus Christ. The things you fear most took their best shots at him; and he defeated them.

That's why it's so important that Mary Magdalene and Joanna and the other women found an empty tomb on that Sunday morning. That's why our faith is founded on the fact that the Jesus who was crucified and buried later rose from the dead in glory and is seated at the right hand of God the Father in heaven. Our salvation is not found in his teaching or his philosophy or his example; if it were, we wouldn't need him to be alive. We could just read about him and his ways.

But Jesus himself *is* our Savior. A dead Jesus couldn't save anyone. But Jesus isn't dead. He's alive right now—and so we can go to him in faith and find salvation. We can find help in our time of need. We can find mercy when we are struggling. We can find grace when we are tempted to sin. We can find comfort when we are afraid. We can know hope in the face of death—even our own death—all because he is not in his tomb; he has risen.

For Reflection:

O *Think back to the time when you became a Christian, or understood your childhood faith for the first time. In what sense were you being shown that you had been wonderfully wrong?*

O *How will knowing that Jesus keeps his promises change the way you're looking at your day today?*

O *"Where else are you going to find a Savior like this?" Where are you tempted to look for alternatives? How will the empty tomb encourage you to look to Christ?*

Jesus lives! Thy terrors now
Can no longer, death, appall us;
Jesus lives! By this we know
Thou, O grave, canst not enthrall us.
Alleluia!

Jesus lives! Henceforth is death
But the gate of life immortal;
This shall calm our trembling breath
When we pass its gloomy portal.
Alleluia!

Jesus lives! For us he died;
Then, alone to Jesus living,
Pure in heart may we abide,
Glory to our Savior giving.
Alleluia!

Jesus lives! our hearts know well
Nought from us his love shall sever;
Life, nor death, nor powers of hell
Tear us from his keeping ever.
Alleluia!

Jesus lives! to him the throne
Over all the world is given:
May we go where he has gone,
Rest and reign with him in heaven.
Alleluia!

"Jesus lives! Thy Terrors Now" by Christian Friedrich Gellert
(translated Frances E. Cox)

CHAPTER TWO

WAS IT NOT NECESSARY?

¹³ Now that same day two of them were going to a village called Emmaus, about seven miles from Jerusalem. ¹⁴ They were talking with each other about everything that had happened. ¹⁵ As they talked and discussed these things with each other, Jesus himself came up and walked along with them; ¹⁶ but they were kept from recognizing him.

¹⁷ He asked them, "What are you discussing together as you walk along?"

They stood still, their faces downcast. ¹⁸ One of them, named Cleopas, asked him, "Are you the only one visiting Jerusalem who does not know the things that have happened there in these days?"

¹⁹ "What things?" he asked.

"About Jesus of Nazareth," they replied. "He was a prophet, powerful in word and deed before God and all the people. ²⁰ The chief priests and our rulers handed him over to be sentenced to death, and they crucified him; ²¹ but we had hoped that he was the one who was going to redeem Israel. And what is more, it is the third day since all this took place. ²² In addition, some of our women amazed us. They went to the tomb early this morning ²³ but didn't find his body. They came and told us that they had seen a vision of angels, who said he was alive. ²⁴ Then some of our companions went to the tomb and found it just as the women had said, but they did not see Jesus."

²⁵ He said to them, "How foolish you are, and how slow to believe all that the prophets have spoken! ²⁶ Did not the Messiah have to suffer these things and then enter his glory?" ²⁷ And beginning with Moses and all the Prophets, he explained to them what was said in all the Scriptures concerning himself.

²⁸ As they approached the village to which they were going, Jesus continued on as if he were going further. ²⁹ But they urged him strongly, "Stay with us, for it is nearly evening; the day is almost over." So he went in to stay with them.

³⁰ When he was at the table with them, he took bread, gave thanks, broke it and began to give it to them. ³¹ Then their eyes were opened and they recognised him, and he disappeared from their sight. ³² They asked each other, "Were not our hearts burning within us while he talked with us on the road and opened the Scriptures to us?"

³³ They got up and returned at once to Jerusalem. There they found the Eleven and those with them, assembled together ³⁴ and saying, "It is true! The Lord has risen and has appeared to Simon." ³⁵ Then the two told what had happened on the way, and how Jesus was recognised by them when he broke the bread.

Luke 24 v 13-35

Recently an American television show sent Matt Harvey, a young "phenom" pitcher for the New York Mets baseball team, out onto the streets of New York to have a little fun. Because Harvey was having a great season, there was a lot of excitement about him among Mets fans. But because this was his first season playing professionally, he didn't have the "face recognition" that more established stars have. So Harvey went around the city with a camera crew and a microphone, stopping people wearing Mets gear and asking them how excited they were about Matt Harvey.

It was funny as people gushed about his abilities and talked about the advice they would give to the young man if they ever met him, only to finally realize that they had been talking to him the whole time. If they had known to whom they were talking, they surely would have been much more measured in their conversation. But because they did not realize to whom they were speaking, they revealed their true, unvarnished thoughts.

Luke is moving us on to the afternoon of the day that changed everything; and he's moved his focus outside the city, to two disciples walking seven miles to Emmaus. They had most likely traveled into the city for the Passover celebration, but now it was time to return to their hometown.

Unsurprisingly, "they were talking with each other about everything that had happened" (v 14). It's unlikely that seven miles would have been enough to talk it all through; but well before Emmaus, they are interrupted by a stranger. A stranger to them, anyway; but we are let in on the secret early—it was "Jesus himself" (v 15). Up to this point, Luke has told us that Jesus has been raised from the dead, but we have not seen him "on camera." Here he is; and it is a little anticlimactic, because no one else in the scene recognizes him! But it does mean that we are hearing these disciples' unvarnished thoughts. As they explain the events and their reactions to this stranger, we are going to see their hearts as they are, not as they would like to present them to their Lord.

What Kind of Redemption?

The disciples probably were not all that thrilled when a stranger joined them on the road and began to pry into the details of their conversation. I know that when something's bothering me, the last thing I want to do is explain it to a stranger. But as they begin to talk with this man on the road, it seems that he's unaware of what's happened over the past few days. So the travelers get their guest caught up to speed by telling him two things. First, they tell him who Jesus was: a prophet who spoke with power and backed it up with mighty actions. Second, they tell him what happened to Jesus: the religious and civil authorities of Israel handed him over to the Romans to be convicted and executed.

And so their overriding emotion is written all over their faces: "downcast" (v 17). You can sense the sadness and bewilderment behind their disillusioned statement: "We had hoped that he was the one who was going to redeem Israel" (v 21). *We had hoped… but we were wrong. We had hoped he… but he couldn't, didn't, won't.* Their hopes had been dashed and they were left to make sense of what had happened; even some amazing and strange reports of Jesus' body disappearing and angels appearing had not shifted their views or their emotions.

But at the heart of their sorrow is a massive misunderstanding of what Jesus had come to do. The word that Cleopas uses, "redeem," is significant. It is a term that is loaded with meaning, and we need to take a minute to try to understand what the disciples mean when they say that they had hoped that Jesus would redeem Israel.

The concept of redemption carried with it the idea of setting someone free from captivity or slavery. When the nation of Israel was suffering as slaves in the land of Egypt, the Lord promised that he would redeem them:

> I am the LORD, and I will bring you out from under the yoke of the Egyptians. I will free you from being slaves to them, and I will redeem you with an outstretched arm and with mighty acts of judgment. (Exodus 6 v 6)

Centuries later, the prophet Isaiah also saw a vision of a day far off in the future when the Christ, God's chosen King, would come walking into the land of Israel in great strength, his garments stained red. When Isaiah asks the Messiah why his clothes are stained in this way, the answer is chilling:

> I have trodden the winepress alone; from the nations no one was with me. I trampled them in my anger and trod them down in my wrath; their

blood spattered my garments, and I stained all my clothing. It was for me the day of vengeance; the year for me to redeem had come.

(Isaiah 63 v 3-4)

This was the scriptural heritage of Israel in the time of the Gospels. And as the New Testament era opened, the nation of Israel was suffering under years of oppressive Roman occupation. It's not surprising, therefore, that there were mounting expectations that the Christ would come soon to bring God's judgment against the enemies of his people. Many, many people in Jerusalem longed to see the King finally come to redeem Israel, especially if it involved getting a little Roman blood on his clothing. When you've been trampled by Roman jackboots for years, the thought of your own Redeemer coming to do some trampling of his own is extremely exciting.

So when you put all of that together, you can see why the disciples on the road to Emmaus were so disappointed. The events that had taken place over the previous few days had been the exact opposite of what they had hoped for from Jesus. Instead of restoring the dignity of Israel, Jesus had been publicly humiliated. Instead of spilling Roman blood in the streets of Jerusalem, Jesus' garments had been soaked in his own blood. Instead of driving the pagan occupiers out of the land, Jesus had been crushed by the Roman machine. After all of that, what hope of redemption could there possibly be for Israel? *We had hoped... but he didn't.*

From where we sit, it may seem fairly easy for us to see where these disciples went wrong. They simply did not understand what it meant for Jesus to redeem Israel. They didn't have a category for a kind of redemption that didn't involve getting rid of their difficult circumstances. They didn't have any idea that there was a kind of redemption that was achieved through weakness and suffering. They couldn't imagine that Jesus was actually redeeming them from captivity to an enemy that was far more oppressive than the Roman Empire. As a result, they could not understand that Jesus' death was not the end of their hopes for redemption. *We had hoped... but he didn't.*

Because they were looking for the wrong kind of redemption, they had totally missed the redemption that had just happened. In fact, Jesus' death *was* the redemption of God's people. He hadn't redeemed them from Roman rule; it turns out that Jesus had much bigger fish to fry. His death redeemed his people by setting them free from both the penalty and power of sin. This invisible power has held mankind in captivity since Adam first rebelled against God. It might not demonstrate its control over us with the same symbols that made Roman oppression an ever-present reality for the Jewish people—sin has no armies and no prisons—but it still holds every human being captive. We cannot help but sin, and we cannot escape the punishment that we deserve for our rebellion against God.

And so the death of Jesus was aimed at freeing us from this enemy. As the apostle Paul put it decades later:

> Christ redeemed us from the curse of the law by becoming a curse for us, for it is written: "Cursed is everyone who is hung on a pole."
>
> (Galatians 3 v 13)

If these men had only understood that they had been redeemed from something far more powerful, far longer-lasting, and far more tyrannical than the Romans, they would have walked down the road with a deep and unshakable joy. Here they were, just days removed from the most wonderful (though sober) event in all of the history of God's dealing with his people, and they were depressed! They were so close to the true source of all joy, but they could not see it—all because they had the wrong expectations.

You and I walk this road, too. Have you ever been disappointed with God? Have you ever felt that God failed to live up to your expectations? Have you started to wonder whether the day-to-day reality of your life reflects the redeeming work of Jesus? Do you have a little voice in your head and heart saying of Christ: "I had hoped he would... but he didn't"?

If so, then I wonder if your disappointment isn't a product of having the wrong expectations of what it means for Jesus to redeem you. We naturally gravitate toward what Martin Luther called a "theology of glory." We expect that if Jesus really makes a difference in our lives, if his redemption and salvation is truly present in us, our lives ought to be marked by peace, strength, uninterrupted growth in holiness, and victory. In short, we expect that things will seem more and more glorious all the time. And when things do not turn out in ways that are consistent with our expectations of glory, we find ourselves disillusioned and downcast. We find ourselves thinking: "I had hoped that Jesus would... but he hasn't."

Or perhaps you have a more practical theology of glory—maybe it seems to you that the *real* problems in your life are practical. You are tired all the time; your house feels too small; your work is mindless and monotonous; your bank account feels as if it is in critical condition, and you've either tried extremely hard to gain a spouse or children, and haven't, or your spouse and children are extremely trying, however hard you try with them. The redemption you long for most of all is freedom right now from those troubles and cares and all of the petty indignities of daily life that make you want to crawl out of your skin. Surely, if Jesus really is good and really is involved, these things ought to be solved? *I had hoped that Jesus would... but he hasn't.*

But that's simply not the salvation that Jesus purchased for us on the cross. Not because those things are too big for him, but because, compared to why he hung there, they're so very small.

We don't tend to hope for too much from Jesus, but too little. He promises the world, beyond death; we demand from him a tweak here and there to our worlds now. He gives us perfect life, forever; we get downcast that our lives now are less than perfect. We set our hearts on a redemption that hasn't been promised, and then get annoyed when God doesn't deliver what he never said he would.

What do you tend to put in the middle of the sentence: "I had hoped that Jesus would... but he hasn't"? That is the place where Jesus is saying to you: *You want a new job, or better health, or a spouse (or a different spouse), or an easier life. How about I give you freedom from fear and hopelessness? How about I give you freedom to be who you are, and be changed into who you were designed to be? How about I give you perfect life for eternity?* The challenge of the Emmaus road is to not reply: "Yeah, thanks for all that, but I'd like a new car, really." Let's be thrilled by the redemption Jesus has brought, not downcast by the redemption he hasn't.

The disciples on the road to Emmaus couldn't see past their blinding pain. They couldn't reconcile their dashed expectations with the idea that perhaps Jesus was bringing them something different, something better. So when you go through periods of disappointment and you are tempted to think that God doesn't care, remember what God has promised you (and what he hasn't!)

The Messiah Had to Suffer

It is interesting to see the way that Jesus responds to these disciples. Unlike the Mets pitcher let loose on an unsuspecting populace, Jesus doesn't mess around with them for his amusement. He corrects them, and his diagnosis of their problem is instructive for us. He tells them that their problem is that they have been slow to believe the prophets. It's a strange comment—how does that connect to what we've seen about the ways that the travelers misunderstood the kind of redemption that Jesus was bringing about?

It turns out that the specific thing that the prophets spoke about, the one thing that Cleopas and his friend didn't believe, was that the Messiah would "have to suffer all these things and then"—only then—"enter his glory" (v 26). You can see how Jesus has put his finger right on the issue: they failed to understand what God's King would be like. Not only had they defined what "glory" would look like (fleeing Romans, victorious Jews)—they had not even begun to get to grips with the fact that suffering had to precede glory. Here the disciples are, wondering how it can be possible that the Messiah would be a victim of such violence, and Jesus comes along and tells them that not only was it possible, it was mandatory! Because that's what God said would happen. God decided that it would be so, and then he went on the record with his intentions. And God had always honored his intentions; Israel's history was a long record of God keeping his promises. Once something was promised by God, it happened.

The Christ's suffering was necessary, and his glory inevitable, because God wanted it to be so. Jesus knew exactly what he would do, because he knew the plan that God had formed before the creation of the world, and had promised before Roman armies ever marched out from Rome (before, in fact, there even was a Rome). If these two men had not been so "slow" to believe the prophets through whom God had laid out his promised plan, they would have understood, too. They would have looked at the cross and seen the Christ suffering, just as God's plan had said. They would have heard of the empty tomb and recognized the Christ's glory, just as God's plan had said.

Hearts on Fire

So what? Well, look at how Cleopas and his companion felt as the Lord Jesus laid out the Old Testament for them, showing them "what was said in all the Scriptures concerning himself" (v 27). Once they had finally had their eyes opened to Jesus' identity, "they asked each other, 'Were not our hearts burning within us while he talked with us on the road and opened the Scriptures to us?'" (v 32).

In other words, the truths Jesus shows them, and us, on this road will set hearts on fire. It will set *your* heart on fire, when you understand that Jesus' death and resurrection bring a greater redemption than you would ever have thought to look for, one that will take you an eternity to appreciate. It will set your heart on fire when you understand that Jesus' death and resurrection are part of a far greater plan than just God's reaction to Israel's issues with the Romans, or your problems today; a plan that began before creation, and involves all of creation. When you realize this is what the resurrection means, it sets your heart on fire.

Many people experience a surge of passion and joy when they first become followers of Christ. This "first love" (Revelation 2 v 4, NIV84 translation) is fueled by a delight in

God's love and the new sensations of freedom from guilt and sin, and certain hope for the future. But let's face it: as time passes, it is easy to let that fade. What was once mind-blowing and heart-burning becomes, well, just "nice." What once sent you to your knees in thanks and opened your mouth in praise now just becomes a background fact, taken for granted. The demands of following Christ can feel like a burden and the sacrifices can seem to outweigh the benefits. The ongoing battle with indwelling sin is discouraging and painful at times. Life goes on, with all its difficulties and disappointments. No wonder the flame of our first love feels as if it is flickering sometimes!

And when that flame flickers, lots of lesser things seem to have a greater ability to make my heart burn within me. I am very passionate about my favorite football team, my family, my favorite music, and so on. Those things take up residence in my heart; they fill my daydreams and my spare time. They thrill me. But I am capable of listening to a sermon, reading the Bible, singing a hymn, and praying to God without much passion at all. It shouldn't be so. I can't help but think that part of my problem is that when I am unmoved by the things of God, the suffering of Christ for me—the great plan of redemption that God has included me in—is not the reality that controls my heart.

If you are like me, take heart. There is good news for people like us: the same kindling that was set on fire in the heart of Cleopas is available to us today. If anything, we have more than they did; from our perch in history we can see further and better. And so there is a standing invitation to you to search the Scriptures and realize that Jesus had to suffer, and did suffer... for you. You can read the Old Testament, read of God's plan to send his Christ to die and rise, and know: "He did that for *me*. He planned to rescue *me*." You can read of the sin and death God has redeemed you from, and the life and future and joy God has redeemed you for, and think: "He has given that to *me*. His death has redeemed *me*." As you do that, you will find your hopes reoriented, given an eternal focus. You won't ask for too little; your disappointments will be put in perspective. You'll find yourself thinking: "My greatest hope is that Christ would enable me to enjoy life with God for ever. *And he has.*"

That is a truth that can set your heart ablaze.

For Reflection:

○ *In what ways are you tempted to look for a different, lesser redemption than the one Jesus came to win for you?*

○ *What difference would a greater grasp of your redemption have on your outlook on your life?*

○ *How will you encourage your heart to be set ablaze by the truths of Christ's suffering and triumph?*

Come, thou long-expected Jesus,
Born to set thy people free;
From our fears and sins release us,
Let us find our rest in thee.
Israel's strength and consolation,
Hope of all the earth thou art;
Dear desire of every nation,
Joy of every longing heart.

Born thy people to deliver,
Born a child and yet a King,
Born to reign in us forever,
Now thy gracious kingdom bring.
By thine own eternal spirit
Rule in all our hearts alone;
By thine all sufficient merit,
Raise us to thy glorious throne.

"Come, Thou Long-Expected Jesus" by Charles Wesley

CHAPTER THREE

THE PEACE
OF CERTAINTY

³⁶ While they were still talking about this, Jesus himself stood among them and said to them, "Peace be with you."

³⁷ They were startled and frightened, thinking they saw a ghost. 38 He said to them, "Why are you troubled, and why do doubts rise in your minds? ³⁹ Look at my hands and my feet. It is I myself! Touch me and see; a ghost does not have flesh and bones, as you see I have."

⁴⁰ When he had said this, he showed them his hands and feet. 41 And while they still did not believe it because of joy and amazement, he asked them, "Do you have anything here to eat?" ⁴² They gave him a piece of broiled fish, ⁴³ and he took it and ate it in their presence.

⁴⁴ He said to them, "This is what I told you while I was still with you: everything must be fulfilled that is written about me in the Law of Moses, the Prophets and the Psalms."

⁴⁵ Then he opened their minds so they could understand the Scriptures. ⁴⁶ He told them, "This is what is written: the Messiah will suffer and rise from the dead on the third day, ⁴⁷ and repentance for the forgiveness of sins will be preached in his name to all nations, beginning at Jerusalem. ⁴⁸ You are witnesses of these things. ⁴⁹ I am going to send you what my Father has promised; but stay in the city until you have been clothed with power from on high."

Luke 24 v 36-49

According to the World Health Agency, by 2015 the citizens of the world will be spending over \$291 billion each year on anti-ageing products. There is a sad irony in that statistic, isn't there? People all over the world are dying from acute causes like malaria and cholera—problems with solutions if only there were the resources to make those solutions available. At the same time, we will spend billions on wrinkle-preventing creams and vitamins to make us feel as if we aren't getting older.

Each of those 291 billion dollars reflects, I think, a deep anxiety that runs below the surface of our culture. The gray hairs and the wrinkles and the paunch remind us that we are getting older. They are signs that life is always growing shorter, that our end always grows ever nearer. And if we are honest, many of us have very little of the emotional equipment necessary to face that reality well. So we spend some money so that we can avoid being reminded of it each time we glance in the mirror.

Westerners are not at peace with the idea of death, and so we go to great lengths to avoid facing it. In centuries gone by, death was a normal (if unpleasant) part of life. Childhood mortality rates were high, women often died in childbirth, and fatal diseases were lurking in the wings. Death was always round the corner. Nowadays, we have beaten back many of these problems. We can pretend that we can prevent the inevitable. But only for a while. Death comes for each and every one of us. We have all lost people that we love, and as much as we might not like to think about it, we all know that one day it will be our turn to die.

So, how can we have peace in a world like this? How can we live with purpose when all our efforts end with us on our deathbed? Is our best plan just to close our eyes, slather on the anti-wrinkle cream, and hope for the best until the worst happens? How can we be calm in the face of the unknown?

Peace at Last

Jesus spent forty days on earth between his resurrection and his return to heaven. Luke records just two of the episodes from those forty days—and this is one of them. His camera lens follows Cleopas and his friend, rushing back to tell the disciples what the women had told them that morning. And then "while they were still talking about this, Jesus himself stood among them" (v 36). Think about the drama as Jesus appears to these followers. What would he say to them? Would he lay into them for abandoning him while he was being crucified? Would he yell at them for not standing with him? Would he vent disgust or disappointment? None of the above! Jesus' first words to his friends after his death and resurrection are: "Peace be with you."

Peace! That word—the Hebrew word *shalom*—was significant to the Jewish way of thinking; it implied wholeness, harmony, and flourishing. Like the English word "peace," *shalom* conveys both the idea of being in right relationship with another (as in, there is peace between my boss and me) and also a sense of overall harmony in our surroundings (as in, I have a wonderful sense of peace when I am out fishing on the river).

When God created the world, it was characterized by *shalom*. Everything in the Garden of Eden flourished. Every relationship was harmonious. Human beings lived at peace with each other, with God, and with the rest of the creation. The world was exactly as it ought to be, exactly as we would want it to be. There was no sorrow, no anxiety, no guilt, and no death. Just take a moment to imagine that world. It's hard, because it's so unlike this one. But it's the one God designed for us to enjoy.

Adam's sin changed all that. As the theologian Cornelius Plantinga has pointed out, one of the fundamental characteristics of sin is that it breaks *shalom*. Sin vandalizes the goodness of creation and introduces discord and strife. If you think about it, all of your problems are the fruit of sin and the brokenness of the world. Everything that makes you feel that you are not living a life of harmony and peace—physical suffering, relational pain and personal failure (yours, and others')—exists because of sin. It is a deeply troubling world, particularly if we understand that, naturally, we are born out of relationship with our Creator.

So when Jesus entered that closed room, his disciples were deeply troubled. They were afraid of the religious leaders that had killed their master. They were plagued with guilt for the way they had let Jesus down in his time of suffering. They were troubled and confused by reports that Jesus had been raised from the dead. And now here he is: the one they deserted, the one they disbelieved. Deeply "troubled" is surely an understatement!

So it is significant, and wonderful, that in his very first words he bids them peace. His death and resurrection have achieved this. On the cross, Jesus absorbed the wrath of God against the sins of his people, taking away everything that prevented there being peace between God and us. In his bodily resurrection, Jesus secured the certain promise that all things would be made new, that we will one day live in a world of perfect peace and harmony. There will certainly be a day when all of the brokenness and pain that sin has caused will be undone. And his appearance in this room shows that Jesus desires to give this peace, even to failing, flawed followers such as them, and such as us.

As followers of Jesus, we can begin to live in that peace now even as we look forward to one day living in it fully and perfectly. Because we are now at peace with God, we can handle difficult relationships at work or in our family in a more peaceful manner. After all, if the most important relationship in my life is marked by peace, that's going to mean that I'm not as affected by difficulties in my less important relationships. I may be having a hard day in this world, but I'm at peace with the One who made this world.

We have peace in difficult relationships, because we know we are at peace with our Maker. We are at peace with our own limitations and sufferings, because we know one day all things will be made new. We are at peace when we do good and when we do wrong, because we know our good deeds do not earn God's love, and our bad ones cannot lose it.

Know For Sure

Of course, this peace is completely grounded in the reality of Christ's resurrection. If we are to experience the peace, we need to be utterly certain about what really happened when Jesus was raised from the dead. After all, the resurrection of Jesus is the one blip on the screen in the long story of human experience with the grave. Billions of people throughout time have been lowered into graves or buried in tombs. So the resurrection of Jesus takes us into uncharted territory.

That seems to be the point that Luke is trying to convey to us in this interaction that Jesus has with his disciples. It is not clear how Jesus got into the room since Luke does not tell us. But we know from the Gospel of John that Jesus was able to enter locked rooms (John 20 v 19) without opening the door. So it seems that after his resurrection Jesus had the ability to appear and disappear at will. That would explain why the disciples were "startled and frightened, thinking they saw a ghost" (Luke 24 v 37)—I think I would come to a similar conclusion if someone suddenly showed up in my office right now without making use of the door!

But in fact Jesus was not a ghost, a point which he demonstrated straight away. Jesus invited the disciples to touch his hands and feet, proving that he was real flesh and bone. He also ate a piece of broiled fish. I don't know much about ghosts, but it seems certain that they don't have bones and they don't eat fish. So the fact that Jesus was not raised from the dead as a ghost was firmly established. He was properly alive, in a proper human body.

Luke is making clear to us not only that Jesus rose, but that he rose physically. And it really matters that the resurrected Jesus wasn't a mere spirit or apparition. It means that Jesus' death really has paid for our sins and defeated our death. If his spirit had been alive but his body had stayed death, his victory would have been partial, and our future would be partial, too. And so it means that we can look forward to resurrection bodies too. Paul describes Jesus as "the firstfruits of those who have fallen asleep" with faith in Christ (1 Corinthians 15 v 20). He is the first part of the harvest: different in timing, but not in type. Jesus has a body that is perfect and eternal; you will, too.

Can you see how someone who is certain about the bodily resurrection of Jesus will be able to experience genuine peace in this world? The things that rob us of peace (guilt, painful relationships, physical weakness, death) are all dealt with in the resurrection of Jesus. We have certain forgiveness, a certain confidence that we will receive new resurrection bodies, and a certain future living in God's presence. That is fertile soil in which a peaceful heart can grow!

Jesus in the Old Testament

But physical evidence isn't everything that Jesus gives. Having eaten the fish, he points them to "everything ... that is written about me"—to the Old Testament—the Law, the Prophets and the Psalms (Luke 24 v 44).

Jesus wanted to talk about the part of the Bible that we now call the Old Testament. That might be a strange place to begin explaining things, but if you follow what Jesus was saying, you'll see why it was important.

Jesus tells us that the entire Old Testament speaks about him. Specifically, Jesus says that it talks about his suffering and resurrection. Now, Jesus isn't saying that every word in the Old Testament is literally about his death and resurrection. But he is telling us that every part of the Old Testament points forward to or prepares God's people for the King who would come to die and rise again for his people. All of the people and patterns and prophecies of the Old Testament find their fulfillment in the death and resurrection of Jesus.

This is a strong incentive for us to study carefully the Old Testament. Too often, Christians read the Old Testament out of obligation, neglect it altogether, or see it as a series of morality stories that tell us what to do and what not to do. Every year, thousands of New Year's resolutions to read through the Bible run aground on the deadly shoals of Leviticus or the genealogies of Chronicles. But if we understand that these books were never meant to be the endpoint of God's revelation—but rather, were supposed to show the character and plans of the Lord, culminating in the coming of his Son and the spread of the gospel to all nations—then we will see meaning and purpose on every page of God's word, not merely the New Testament.

The Bible functions a bit like a complex mystery novel. In those books, the first part of the book is full of clues—

some obvious, some not. Then, toward the end, the mystery is solved. The clues come together in a way that you (well, I) would never manage to predict; but once they do, it's all obvious! You suddenly realize the point of the seemingly random events that came before. So you can't fully understand the end without the beginning—but you can't confidently understand the beginning without the end.

In the same way, you will never grasp what is going on in the Gospels and the rest of the New Testament if you don't read them with the Old Testament in mind. Take one simple example: how do you know why it matters that Jesus is the Christ if you don't know what God has promised about the Christ? But equally, the way you can get to grips with the Old Testament is to read it all as pointing to the climax, to the solving of the mystery to which all the clues are pointing you: the life, death and resurrection of Jesus the Christ. Knowing him is the key that unlocks the Old Testament.

If we understand how the Old Testament points forward to Jesus, it will help give us confidence in the reality of his death and resurrection. They were not ideas dreamed up by the disciples; it was not a divine afterthought. The evidence of that room, and the evidence of the Scriptures, can give great certainty that Jesus really rose—and can give great confidence that, right now, in all the ups and downs of your life, through all your fears and failures, Jesus says to you: "Peace be with you."

Hidden Meaning

But there is a twist. After hearing about the empty tomb, seeing the risen Lord Jesus, and having a Bible study with the One the Bible is all about, these guys still don't get it!

The disciples were good Jews; they probably knew their Scriptures much better than we do (after all, they didn't have internet videos of adorable cats to clog up the storage space in their brains!) Not only that, but they had spent three years living with Jesus, the greatest Bible teacher of all time. Yet, at the end of verse 44, they are still unable to grasp what they are seeing and hearing. They are still unable to hear that the risen Christ's peace is for them.

This is pretty par for the course with the disciples. Earlier in his Gospel, Luke tells us about a time when Jesus made everything abundantly clear to his disciples, but they still weren't able to make heads or tails of it:

> Jesus took the Twelve aside and told them, "We are going up to Jerusalem, and everything that is written by the prophets about the Son of Man will be fulfilled. He will be delivered over to the Gentiles. They will mock him, insult him and spit on him; they will flog him and kill him. On the third day he will rise again." The disciples did not understand any of this. Its meaning was hidden from them, and they did not know what he was talking about.   (Luke 18 v 31-34)

It doesn't get much more explicit than that. Sometimes in his earthly ministry Jesus was pretty subtle and it was hard to grasp his meaning. But this isn't one of those times; Jesus is perfectly clear but still his hearers don't understand. Why? Because "its meaning was hidden from them." Their problem wasn't intellectual; it was spiritual.

Even by the time of Luke 24, the disciples still can't get it. They need Jesus to do what he does in verse 45: "He opened their minds so they could understand the Scriptures" that point to him and explain his death and resurrection. The fact is, you cannot be open-minded about Christ unless your mind is opened by Christ.

You see, there is a difference between merely reading the words of the Bible and truly understanding in your heart and mind what they mean. This is why you can explain the good news about Jesus to someone who doesn't believe, and they just can't see what you see in it. This is why you can give someone good biblical counsel, but they just don't seem to be able to see that they should follow it. This is why (if you can remember becoming a Christian) you can look back on a time when what now seems very obvious was only thoroughly confusing. We needed—we still need—the work of Christ, through his Spirit—"the Spirit who is from God ... that we may understand what God has freely given us" (1 Corinthians 2 v 12). He is the only one who can give us eyes to see the risen Jesus, and hear his words as being for us, changing our minds and hearts and perspective and future: "Peace be with you."

This truth should make us *humble*. If you have any insight into the Scriptures or any knowledge of God, it is not due to anything you can take credit for. If you have taken to reading the Scriptures without praying first, remember that you will not understand through your own willpower or brainpower, but only through the Spirit's mind-opening power. Our need for illumination reminds us that we are dependent on the risen Jesus at every turn for our spiritual life, and it also reminds us that he is responsible for every good spiritual thing in our lives.

This truth should also make us *prayerful*. If you hope to see a loved one come to love Jesus someday, you will need him to open their eyes. That fact should drive us to prayer. And it should make us *bold*. Ultimately, the effectiveness of your witness to other people doesn't depend on the cleverness of your words or the brilliance of your presentation of the gospel message. No one can come to Jesus unless God opens their eyes to understand; but anyone can come to Christ if he does, and enjoy the peace that a dying world cannot find anywhere else.

Friend, are you at peace with your Maker? God extends forgiveness and reconciliation to anyone who will lay down their rebellious arms and come to him through faith in his Son. If you have never known that peace, ask God to open your eyes today.

And if you have received that forgiveness and grace, have they made you a peaceful person? Do you fear growing older? Can you weather the storms of daily life with a calm demeanor? When life gets tough, can you look forward with anticipation to being with Christ forever? Do you let Christ's peace make a difference when you feel startled or frightened?

Someone once said of the great theologian Jonathan Edwards, when he was experiencing a great time of difficulty, that "his peace was beyond the reach of any man." Edwards' peace came from his certainty that his Savior was alive, and that as a result this life is not the end of the story. May that same peace be yours!

For Reflection:

O *How do you view ageing and death? What difference does, or should, the resurrection make to it?*

O *How can the reality of your peace with God spill over into how you deal with difficult relationships?*

O *How will knowing that only Jesus can enable you to see the truth make you more humble and more prayerful?*

Far away in the depths of my spirit tonight
Rolls a melody sweeter than psalm;
In celestial strains it unceasingly falls
O'er my soul like an infinite calm.

What a treasure I have in this wonderful peace,
Buried deep in the heart of my soul,
So secure that no power can mine it away,
While the years of eternity roll!

I am resting tonight in this wonderful peace,
Resting sweetly in Jesus' control;
For I'm kept from all danger by night and by day,
And His glory is flooding my soul!

Peace, peace, wonderful peace,
Coming down from the Father above!
Sweep over my spirit forever, I pray
In fathomless billows of love!

"Wonderful Peace" by Warren D. Cornell (Verses 1 to 3 and Chorus)

CHAPTER FOUR

THE PARTING

⁵⁰ When he had led them out to the vicinity of Bethany, he lifted up his hands and blessed them. ⁵¹ While he was blessing them, he left them and was taken up into heaven. ⁵² Then they worshipped him and returned to Jerusalem with great joy. ⁵³ And they stayed continually at the temple, praising God.

Luke 24 v 50-53

You might not even notice it, but throughout your day you are surrounded by places that you are not permitted to enter. Signs at the hardware store tell you that a certain area is for "Employees Only." The entire force of the nation's military seems ready to pounce on you if you even think about entering a restricted zone at the airport. If you go to a sporting event or a concert or a club, certain areas are simply off-limits to ordinary people like you and me. We aren't allowed to get too close to the athletes or the musicians; we can't go where the VIPs go.

Most of the time, this isn't a big deal. But there are some situations in life where it would be great to be "on the other side of the rope." A few times a year, I find myself on an overnight flight. I'm moderately tall, and so the seats in coach class, which seem to be designed for children and people who are amputated above the knee, become uncomfortable after about an hour. At the three-hour mark, when the person in front of me inevitably reclines his seat into my lap, I begin to stare longingly beyond the gauzy curtain in the aisle, into the promised land of first class. Up there, on the other side, there's space and comfort. Up in first class, no one climbs over you in the middle of the night to get to the lavatory. But alas, first class is not for people like me.

But I like to imagine how it would change things if I had a close friend on the inside. What if my best friend were a flight attendant on my plane? For that matter, what if they were the stage manager for the theater or a roadie for my favorite band? That would be a different story altogether, wouldn't it? If you had a friend on the inside, then they could get you access. Having somebody on the inside would make all the difference.

Well, the good news from the end of the Gospel of Luke is that we have a friend in the most exclusive, most wonderful place ever. We have someone looking out for us in the throne-room of heaven itself. That is the meaning of Jesus' ascension into heaven: you have got the closest of friends in the first-class section of the universe.

What Happened?

To be honest, I find Luke's account of Jesus' return to heaven—referred to as "the ascension"—almost maddeningly brief! This is a man who spent five verses describing how John the Baptist got his name (1 v 59-63), but all we get here is nine words: "He left them and was taken up into heaven" (24 v 51). I do not know about you, but that leaves me with questions! What does it mean that he was taken up into heaven? By whom? On what? What did it look like? Was it fast, as if there was a jetpack strapped to his back? Or kind of slow, with lots of waving and time to say goodbye? Were there angels involved? Were there sound effects—trumpets blaring and that kind of thing? Luke just says: "He left them and was taken up into heaven"!

Whatever questions we may have, Luke's account is inspired by the Holy Spirit, so we can be sure that we have been told everything that is good for us to know about what happened. And in fact, if we look closely at Luke's nine words, we see three important facts emerge about the ascension.

First, Jesus *ascended*. OK, I admit that one is kind of obvious; Luke does not say that when Jesus left the disciples, he just walked out of view or jumped into the sea. Luke tells us that he was "taken up."

Second, Jesus ascended *bodily*. We've already seen that Jesus proved to the disciples that he was *physically* raised from the dead. He had them put their hands in his wounds. He ate fish to prove that he was not a ghost. As he stands there with his disciples at Bethany, Jesus still has his resurrected body. And as he is taken up, Luke does not tell us that Jesus shed his flesh and became a disembodied soul. We do not read that a physical shell came hurtling back to earth and Jesus' spirit was taken up. There is no tomb except the empty one. Jesus ascended with a physical body and he remains in his physical, glorified resurrection body to this day.

Third, Jesus ascended bodily *into heaven*. This is one of the few details that Luke gives us; he tells us that Jesus was taken up into heaven. Now, there are a lot of things about heaven that we do not understand, but this vital piece of information give us some clues. Because Jesus has a body, subject to spatial limitations, and because that body went into heaven, heaven must be a real place, not just a state of mind. So while we can't see heaven and we don't know where it is exactly (though "up" reminds us that no one has managed to build it on earth, despite the promises of various revolutionaries and romantics), we can be sure that it exists and Jesus is there.

This is an extraordinary truth. After Adam and Eve sinned against God, humanity was cast out of God's presence (Genesis 3 v 22-24). But now Jesus, with his full humanity still intact, has entered into heaven. He lives in the presence of his Father, receiving the worship of the heavenly host.

But even more extraordinary is the fact that Jesus has gone into the throne room of the universe and will bring us to be there with him. This is the beauty of what Jesus has done for us. He belongs in heaven; it fits with his perfection and dignity and glory. But he left those surroundings in order to bring us to be with him (2 Corinthians 8 v 9). By virtue of his death and resurrection, Jesus has made it so that we can be welcomed into heaven. He has washed us clean from the sin and guilt that disqualifies us from entrance into heaven. He gives us his righteousness as a gift so that we can stand in the presence of God with great joy (Jude v 24).

That seems almost too good to be true. Jesus, the Son of God from all eternity, is in the presence of God in heaven right now—not for his own sake, but for yours. All humanity fell into sin and death because of the work of Adam; but in Jesus we find a human representative who lifts us up to the throne room of heaven. Jesus is the second Adam, who did everything he did on our behalf. He lived and died and rose and even ascended into heaven for us. We have a friend "on the inside" of heaven, looking out for our interests.

So What?

With that fact firmly planted in our minds, we are ready to ask the next question: how does the fact that Jesus is in heaven change the way that we live? Later today, I will meet with a couple whose marriage is in crisis. What difference does it make to them that Jesus is in heaven right now? Today, you will probably deal with all kinds of stresses and anxieties, fears and problems. You will (hopefully) have joys and pleasure as well. How do we face those things differently in light of the fact that Jesus is in the throne room of heaven? In our passage we see two ways that the first disciples responded to Jesus' ascension.

Worship and Praise

When Jesus ascended to heaven, he did not take up a position of lowliness, service or humility. There was a time for that during his earthly ministry; he came to be "among you as one who serves" (Luke 22 v 27). But that is in the past; Jesus is now exalted over the angels and seated like a king at the right hand of God in heaven (theologians refer to this as Christ's session). Jesus is "seated ... at [God's] right hand in the heavenly realms, far above all rule and authority, power and dominion, and every name that is invoked" (Ephesians 1 v 20-21).

As a result, the first thing that the disciples did after Jesus' departure was to worship him. It was the only appropriate response; when a king is crowned, those present kneel to demonstrate their loyalty and submission to his authority. What else besides worship could begin to do justice to an event like Jesus' return to heavenly glory?

Today, there are a lot of things vying for our worship; our hearts and the world around us bombard us with potential idols. It is easy to fall into living for the approval of an employer or spouse. We might be tempted to make finances or success or family or our physical appearance the thing that controls our time and emotional state. But none of those things are worthy of our worship like Jesus. None of those things should be on the throne of our hearts. None of those things deserve to be seated next to the Majesty in heaven.

So the next time you are tempted to worship something else with your love and life, remember that there is One who has ascended to heaven. He is wearing the crown of the universe. Heaven revolves around him; the earth revolves because of him. If he will not be the center of your life and your affections, who or what will be? Are these things being worshiped right now by millions of angels? Have they been exalted by the Father? When you put it that way, they all look like sad and pathetic little substitutes for Jesus. We only have one King who is worthy of worship.

This explains why, according to Luke, the disciples spent their days in the temple praising God. Who else would they praise? God had sent his Son to save them. All they had contributed was confusion and desertion.

The Joy of a Human in Heaven

The disciples' other response to the ascension was joy. Despite the fact that their friend and master was gone, they returned to Jerusalem with joy in their hearts. And once they were there, they spent their time in the temple praising God for what he had done for them.

There is a lot to be joyful about when we contemplate Christ's ascension into heaven. When we think about Jesus in heaven, we can enjoy knowing for sure that God loves us. It is hard enough to imagine the love that motivated God's Son to take on human flesh. In Jesus, God has stepped into our world. He has taken up residence among us, spoken our language, and adopted our customs. The Son of God knows what it is like to have flesh and bones, and to make speech using lungs and lips and a tongue. He became one of us.

But that's not the end of the story. I would have expected that the Son of God would want to dump his humanity as soon as possible, kicking it off at the doorway of heaven like we might kick off muddy boots before entering the house. Being a human hadn't been the easiest part of the Son's eternal existence. Once he had lived his more than thirty years as a man, died on the cross for the sins of humans, and then had risen from the dead in victory over the sin and death that have held humanity prisoner, Jesus would have been well within his rights to divest himself of any trappings of his humanity. I would have expected him to go back to heaven and resume an existence similar to the one he enjoyed before he took on flesh.

But that is not what Jesus did. When the Son of God became a man, he did so for all eternity. Forever and ever, the second person of the Trinity will be a human being. That's powerful evidence that God loves humanity. If something repulses you, you would not invite it to stay in your presence. If a rat wandered into your kitchen, you probably would not welcome it in and ask it to stay for all eternity. So the very fact that God's plan was for humanity to be represented in his presence forever shows God's love for and commitment to humanity. That's an excellent reason to have joy!

The Joy of Your Welcome in Heaven

We should also have joy because the ascension of Christ is not only good news globally—for humanity—but personally—for you. Jesus' position in heaven means that you will one day be welcomed into the presence of God. Every good action story has a scene where the hero must enter into some scary place where no rational person would ever dream of going (think Bilbo heading into Smaug's cave in *The Hobbit,* or Ethan Hunt hacking a CIA computer while suspended from cables in the ceiling in *Mission Impossible*). The tension rises as the hero risks everything by trespassing onto an enemy's territory.

Well, in the Bible the scariest place for sinners to be is in the presence of a holy God. There is something about the purity and holiness of God that sinners cannot bear. If we had to depend on our work or our goodness in order to be welcomed by God, we would have cause only for despair, not joy.

But the ascension of Jesus into heaven changes all of that for us. Those who are believers are "in Christ," new creations who have received the righteousness of Jesus as a gift (2 Corinthians 5 v 17-21). This means that if Jesus is righteous enough to be in the presence of God, so am I. Not because I am personally holy and sinless, but because I am united to Jesus, and so when God looks on me he counts Jesus' righteousness as mine.

This is why people who know Jesus need not approach God with terror and panic. We don't need to fear that God will not hear our prayers because we have sinned. We do not need to worry that some day we will get to heaven and someone will say: "Sinners like you do not belong here!" Jesus is there for us, a sympathetic representative for God's people, and so we can always go to God with boldness and confidence that we have not earned.

Have you noticed that the idea of joy keeps coming up in Luke's narrative of Jesus' resurrection and ascension? In fact, at every major stage of Jesus' time on earth recorded in his Gospel, Luke mentions people responding with joy. When Mary becomes pregnant with God's Son, the unborn prophet John the Baptist jumps for joy (1 v 44), while Mary herself rejoices (v 47). Christ's birth is announced by angels as "good news that will cause great joy" (2 v 10). When Jesus' first followers go out on mission to share the gospel, they return with joy (10 v 17). On Palm Sunday, as the King enters his capital city, the crowd with him joyfully praise God (19 v 37). And joy was a feature of the disciples' reaction to meeting the crucified, risen Jesus (24 v 40-41).

Joy is what happens when you meet with Jesus as your Lord and Savior. Joy is what happens when you grasp who he is, why he came, and where he is now. It's almost like a test of whether or not you really understand what's going on in the story. These are not events that are meant to stay confined to our heads; they are meant to percolate down into our hearts and change the way we think, feel, and love. So ask yourself: *Do I know great joy?*

If not, I'm sympathetic. Life is hard. Even the smoothest ride on this earth is marked by suffering, heartache and loss. Many people in today's western world live at standards of health and prosperity that would have been unimaginable for 99.9% of the people who have ever lived on earth, but we still aren't free from depression and loneliness and weakness. The happiest lives all end in the grave. There are a lot of reasons not to be happy on a day-to-day basis. If we tie our deep-down sense of well-being to our circumstances, joy will be elusive.

Christian joy is different. It is built on knowing Christ, not remolding our circumstances. The fact that Jesus is in heaven at this moment gives us a hope that transcends our daily troubles; because if Jesus is in heaven, then we will one day surely be with him there. The frustrations and sorrows of daily life are not the final word. They punctuate our story now, but they are not the story itself. And one day, they will be behind us.

Perhaps if we lack joy, it is because our thoughts are too focused on the here and now, and not focused enough on heaven. Sometimes people are criticized for being "heavenly minded." But actually it's good to be heavenly minded. We should think about heaven every day, because Jesus is there right now. We should feel free to look forward to heaven, because it is our eternal home. Our forefathers (and foremothers) in the faith knew this—they wrote hymns to encourage believers to long for heaven. But it seems as if our generation of believers sometimes feel that if they think about heaven too much, then they are escapists who cannot cope with the fact that life is hard.

The fact is, most of us don't long for heaven *enough*. And that means our lives here on earth don't reflect that citizenship above. We don't live as though our lives are hidden with Christ on high. We don't live as if we're heading there to live with the ascended Jesus. Instead, we live as if the financial difficulties, the relationship struggles, and the family concerns in our lives are the final reality. It's no wonder that we struggle to feel joy.

We need to lift our gaze. We need to look up—up to where Jesus sits on his throne, for us. We need to look forward—forward to where Jesus will one day welcome us into his presence to share his glory. We need to reflect on his incarnation, and know that he came for us. We need to wonder at his birth, and see that he humbled himself for us. We need to look at his mission, and understand that he came to reach us. We need to gaze at his kingship, and know that he rules for us. We need to know that he rose to life, scarred but not defeated by his death, for us. Today, look up to your Friend in heaven; look forward to seeing your Friend in heaven. That's how you worship with great joy. It is good to have a friend on the inside!

For Reflection:

○ *How has this chapter encouraged you in your prayers?*

○ *Where do you tend to look for joy? How will you remember to find joy in knowing that Christ has ascended?*

○ *Are you looking forward to heaven? How can you be more heavenly minded?*

Look, ye saints, the sight is glorious;
See the Man of Sorrows now!
From the fight returned victorious,
Every knee to him shall bow.
Crown him! Crown him!
Crowns become the victor's brow.

Crown the Savior! Angels, crown him!
Rich the trophies Jesus brings;
On the seat of power enthrone him
While the vault of heaven rings.
Crown him! Crown him!
Crown the Savior King of kings.

Sinners in derision crowned him,
Mocking thus the Savior's claim;
Saints and angels crowd around him,
Own his title, praise his name.
Crown him! Crown him!
Spread abroad the victor's fame!

Hark, those bursts of acclamation!
Hark, those loud triumphant chords!
Jesus takes the highest station;
Oh, what joy the sight affords!
Crown him! Crown him!
King of kings and Lord of lords!

"Look, Ye Saints, The Sight Is Glorious" by Thomas Kelly

CHAPTER FIVE

LEAVING TO RETURN

[1] In my former book, Theophilus, I wrote about all that Jesus began to do and to teach [2] until the day he was taken up to heaven, after giving instructions through the Holy Spirit to the apostles he had chosen. [3] After his suffering, he presented himself to them and gave many convincing proofs that he was alive. He appeared to them over a period of forty days and spoke about the kingdom of God. [4] On one occasion, while he was eating with them, he gave them this command: "Do not leave Jerusalem, but wait for the gift my Father promised, which you have heard me speak about. [5] For John baptised with water, but in a few days you will be baptised with the Holy Spirit."

[6] Then they gathered round him and asked him, "Lord, are you at this time going to restore the kingdom to Israel?"

[7] He said to them: "It is not for you to know the times or dates the Father has set by his own authority. [8] But you will receive power when the Holy Spirit comes on you; and you will be my witnesses in Jerusalem, and in all Judea and Samaria, and to the ends of the earth."

[9] After he said this, he was taken up before their very eyes, and a cloud hid him from their sight.

[10] They were looking intently up into the sky as he was going, when suddenly two men dressed in white stood beside them. [11] "Men of Galilee," they said, "why do you stand here looking into the sky? This same Jesus, who has been taken from you into heaven, will come back in the same way you have seen him go into heaven."

Acts 1 v 1-11

Imagine that you were going on a trip and you were not going to see your loved ones for a very long time. What would you say to them? With limited time, what would you leave ringing in the ears of your spouse? Your children? Your parents? Your best friend?

Whatever you say, it will need to get them through the coming period of your absence. They will, doubtless, remember these words and roll them over and over in their minds whenever they think about you. Surely you would want to assure them of your love and that they will be in your thoughts. Perhaps you would want to give your children advice to get them through life without you.

Final words matter. Something about knowing that you won't get another chance, that you will not have an opportunity to clarify or add to what you have said, gives final words extra importance. In Acts, Luke's second volume, he picks up where he left off at the end of his Gospel; in fact, he overlaps the beginning of Acts with the end of Luke a little bit. And whereas the Gospel of Luke begins with Jesus' birth, the book of Acts begins with his final words before he leaves his disciples for a long time.

This chapter opens in the middle of an extraordinary forty-day period in human history. For forty days after his resurrection, Jesus met with his apostles and helped them to understand what had happened to him, and what was about to happen after he ascended into heaven.

So, what was it that Jesus wanted his followers to do? Now that Jesus had been crucified and raised from the dead, what was the first step in the big plan that was about to be unleashed on the world? Well, in a word: wait. Jesus tells them that there is nothing for them to do at the moment; they need to wait in Jerusalem until they are baptized in the Holy Spirit. Only at that point can they do anything; until then they must wait.

Baptism with the Holy Spirit must have sounded very exciting. What did it mean? The disciples thought they knew: "Lord, are you at this time going to restore the kingdom to Israel?" (v 6). After everything that had happened, it seems that they still expected that Jesus was going to bring a political and even military rule; that the Roman authorities would be defeated and the ancient borders of Israel would be re-established. Those hopes had been crushed when Jesus was crucified; it seems they'd been re-ignited when he rose from the dead.

But Jesus quickly dismisses their questions. There will come a day when he will return from heaven and the world's systems and governments all will be publicly brought under the authority of Christ (Revelation 11 v 15). But the timing of that event "is not for you to know" (Acts 1 v 7). The Christian life is not about having all the answers; it is about knowing that there is One who does.

What the disciples do need to know is that their horizons are far too small. They want the kingdom to come to Israel; but Jesus is going to take it to the entire world... through them. They want political and military power; but Jesus is going to give them spiritual power.

Going Viral

Where will Jesus be King? Jesus says at the end of Acts 1 v 8 that the message about his death and resurrection will spread from Jerusalem to Judea and Samaria and then into all the earth. That describes a steady expansion out from the city (Jerusalem) to the region (Judea and Samaria) and then into the entire world. As the book of Acts unfolds,

Luke's narrative will roughly follow this geographical description. At first, the disciples preach the gospel in Jerusalem (chapters 1 – 7). Then persecution spreads the church out to Judea, the surrounding area, and into Samaria, a nearby state (chapters 8 – 12). Then finally we see the gospel going out into the rest of the world, ultimately reaching all the way to Rome, the center of the world at that time (chapters 13 – 28).

From the outset, the message about Jesus has something like a built-in centrifugal force; it is a message that must spread. It cannot be contained. That's the story that the book of Acts tells. Once the gospel story is unleashed on the world, people keep becoming followers of Christ and then head out to spread the word all over the world. The entire enterprise just keeps growing and spreading, despite the best efforts of all of its enemies. Sometimes, their best efforts even serve its spread. It grows from a few people in Jerusalem to thousands of people in the region to millions of people all over the world.

Acts tells us the story of an unstoppable force spreading over the globe. If you are a Christian and you do not live in Jerusalem, you are proof of its power! The message has reached all the way to you, wherever you are. Jesus had you in mind as he spoke his final words to his first followers.

The Messengers

There are a lot of different ways to spread a message these days. Technology allows us to email, tweet, or post information that can be seen on the other side of the world in an instant. But the good news about the death and resurrection and ascension of Jesus spread in a much more analog fashion: Jesus told his disciples that they would be his witnesses. They would simply go and tell the world.

It is a surprisingly simple plan. The disciples do not have any experience in marketing. They are not experts in public relations. They just have a story to tell; a story that they witnessed with their own eyes, a story that could change people's lives. And that is exactly what they did; they proclaimed to the world the things that they had seen and heard from Jesus (1 John 1 v 3), and more and more people became Christians.

As the book of Acts unfolds, we see Jesus' words fulfilled in a surprising way. It turns out that it is not just the apostles who will be Jesus' witnesses, but "ordinary" Christians like you and me are drafted into the work. The message about Jesus has the power to make its hearers into messengers!

This strategy has not changed in 2,000 years. The apostles are gone and the church is no longer centralized in Jerusalem, but God still employs messengers to spread the good news. And that is where you and I come in. We are witnesses to the gospel. We are engaged in Christ's great plan to bring his message "to the ends of the earth." We are not just to be gospel hearers; we are to be gospel sharers, too.

That means that even the "normal" Christian life is really a thrilling adventure. It doesn't matter if you don't have the most exciting "day job;" whether you are a CEO or a stay-at-home mom, or even if you've been out of work for a while, you wake up every morning with an assignment that has eternal significance. God could simply zap people and make them Christians, but instead he gives you and me the joy and privilege of being involved.

Think about the places that you will go today: your home, your neighborhood, your office, the gathering places for your community. Peter and John and James aren't going to show up there today. I've never seen them at my daughter's softball game or at the coffee shop in my town. So chances are, if someone is going to tell the people there about what Jesus has done, it is going to be you and me. Wherever your day takes you, take the gospel there!

The Power for the Mission

How do you feel about the job Jesus gave you? The thought of witnessing probably stresses you out a bit. At best, it's a duty to be endured; often, it's a draft to be dodged. It certainly doesn't feel like a privilege to be embraced! Evangelism is intimidating; if we are honest, it feels like a lot of personal risk for a pretty unlikely result. What have you got? A message. That's it.

That's all the disciples had, too. Remember, these are the same guys we met in the Gospel of Luke. Flawed, doubting, worrying, fearful. And yet they did it; they witnessed, even when it cost them their lives. And the strategy worked; the gospel spread without weapons, without armies, without money, without all of the things that normally signify power and persuasion in our world. It defies logic. How did these ordinary men do it? By what power did these unimpressive witnesses turn the world upside down (as the people of Thessalonica complained in Acts 17 v 6)?

The answer is: the Holy Spirit. Jesus promised them "power when the Holy Spirit comes on you" (v 8). Jesus asks great things of his followers; but he does not ask anything that he does not give them the ability to do. As the book of Acts progresses, the Holy Spirit empowers the mission of the church in several different ways:

- *He gives believers boldness.* The Spirit's power makes men and women fearless in their proclamation of the gospel (4 v 31).

- *He leads believers to people who need the gospel.* The Spirit directs believers to specific individuals (8 v 29) or cities (16 v 6 -10) in need of the gospel message.

- *He gives new life to people who hear the gospel.* If it were not for the Spirit's work, sinners would never be able to embrace and believe the gospel. The only way someone can respond to the message is if the Spirit opens his or her heart (eg: 16 v 14).

Jesus did not send his people out to witness about him without giving them the power they needed for the task. When he ascended, Jesus sent his Spirit to provide them with the courage, wisdom and power that they were lacking. That's the only explanation for the effectiveness of the apostles. They were not brilliant marketers or salesmen; they were simply witnesses to the death, resurrection and ascension of Jesus who were set on fire by God's Spirit. When we think about the task of reaching the world today with the gospel message, too often we get caught up in thinking about what would seem impressive or attractive to the world. But that was never Jesus' plan. His way of doing mission has been simple and unimpressive from day one. He makes disciples, not headlines. Strategies are fine and programs can be useful, but what we really need more than anything else is the power of the Holy Spirit moving through faithful witnesses.

The Game-Changing Spirit

The power of the Holy Spirit working in and through us— the divine involvement in the mission of witnessing—is what changes the game. It means the gospel message is not fragile and weak; its success is not in doubt and it is not hanging by a thread. It means the spread of the gospel does not depend on us being clever and attractive enough to compel people to come to Jesus. The power for spreading the gospel does not come from us. When you witness, there is more power involved in opening your mouth and opening others' hearts than you could ever appreciate.

Jesus' commission calls us; his Holy Spirit empowers and encourages us; as we see the gospel spreading through Acts, it should thrill us; and all these things completely eradicate our excuses. Why do I fail to witness? It is usually because I think it is too hard; or because I think it won't work (or both!) We're tempted to read the book of Acts and think it must have been wonderful to be part of that time in the church's history—a time when thousands repented, when amazing things happened all the time, when things were hopping as the gospel spread all over the place.

But stop to think about what the first disciples faced: they were just eleven ordinary guys in a city that had just murdered their leader. The most powerful people in town all wanted to wipe out their movement. The crowds had shouted for Christ's execution. And Jesus had just gone back to heaven. Eleven men, with a world to witness to—a world that hated them. And you think you have a difficult job in our day, in your corner of the world?!

It is not harder for us; and it is the same Spirit working through us. Yes, our circumstances are different; perhaps it is true that the Spirit's work is less obvious and dramatic now than it was in the ministry of the apostles. But he has grown no less powerful to save sinners in the past 2,000 years. The Holy Spirit is just as committed to the spread of the gospel and the glory of Christ now as he was in those days. We can be sure that the Spirit will give us the boldness, guidance, and grace that we need to carry out the task of evangelism. If you are a reluctant witness, why don't you begin by asking God's Spirit to give you one opportunity this week to tell someone about Jesus? Then ask him to give you the boldness to open your mouth and the wisdom to speak wisely. And then when that happens, pray that God would open the eyes of that person's heart so that they can believe. The power of the Spirit makes all the difference!

Gone to Return

Last words mean a lot. And for Jesus, the last words that he spoke to his disciples before his ascension were nothing less than a global evangelism plan that would be carried out over the next couple of thousand years, and counting. And then he left, taken up before their eyes into heaven.

Unsurprisingly, they stood there, "looking intently up into the sky as he was going" (1 v 10)—you would, wouldn't you?! But they shouldn't have. That's what the angels (perhaps the same ones who spoke to the women at the empty tomb) come to explain. "Jesus ... will come back in the same way you have seen him go into heaven" (v 11). And, once the Holy Spirit had come days later, there was work to do. There was a world to witness to.

We live between Pentecost, when the Spirit came, and the day when Christ will "come back in the same way." We live waiting for him to return. But we do not wait by waiting around. Jesus' departure was a call to action. So, how will you spend your time between now and that day?

It will be very easy to sit in a huddle with other Christians, hunkering down and waiting around. It will be very easy to notice that it is hard to witness, and decide it is too hard for you to witness. It will be very easy to forget the power that is available to you, and decide you are too stuttering, or unknowledgeable, or whatever, for your witnessing to have an impact. It will be far harder, but far more exciting, and far more eternally significant, to get on with it. The ends of the earth are still to be reached—you live in them. The mission continues—join in! Jesus has gone to heaven; and Jesus is coming back. Until then, we wait by witnessing.

For Reflection:

○ *How do you feel about the part God is calling you to play in his mission?*

○ *How much of a game-changer do you see the Holy Spirit as in your life and witness?*

○ *How has this chapter either encouraged you in your evangelism, or challenged you to begin with some evangelism?*

O for a thousand tongues to sing
My great Redeemer's praise,
The glories of my God and King,
The triumphs of his grace!

My gracious Master and my God,
Assist me to proclaim,
To spread through all the earth abroad
The honors of thy name.

Jesus! the name that charms our fears,
That bids our sorrows cease;
'Tis music in the sinner's ears,
'Tis life, and health, and peace.

He speaks, and listening to his voice,
New life the dead receive;
The mournful, broken hearts rejoice,
The humble poor believe.

Hear him, ye deaf; his praise, ye dumb,
your loosened tongues employ;
ye blind, behold your savior come,
and leap, ye lame, for joy.

"O For a Thousand Tongues to Sing" by Charles Wesley
(verses 1 to 3, 5 to 6)

CHAPTER SIX

A NEW
WITNESS

¹² Then the apostles returned to Jerusalem from the hill called the Mount of Olives, a Sabbath day's walk from the city. ¹³ When they arrived, they went upstairs to the room where they were staying. Those present were Peter, John, James and Andrew; Philip and Thomas, Bartholomew and Matthew; James son of Alphaeus and Simon the Zealot, and Judas son of James. ¹⁴ They all joined together constantly in prayer, along with the women and Mary the mother of Jesus, and with his brothers.

¹⁵ In those days Peter stood up among the believers (a group numbering about a hundred and twenty) ¹⁶ and said, "Brothers and sisters, the Scripture had to be fulfilled in which the Holy Spirit spoke long ago through David concerning Judas, who served as guide for those who arrested Jesus. ¹⁷ He was one of our number and shared in our ministry."

¹⁸ (With the payment he received for his wickedness, Judas bought a field; there he fell headlong, his body burst open and all his intestines spilled out. ¹⁹ Everyone in Jerusalem heard about this, so they called that field in their language Akeldama, that is, Field of Blood.)

²⁰ "For," said Peter, "it is written in the Book of Psalms:

"'May his place be deserted;
   let there be no one to dwell in it,'

and,

"'May another take his place of leadership.'

²¹ Therefore it is necessary to choose one of the men who have been with us the whole time the Lord Jesus was living among us, ²² beginning from John's baptism to the time when Jesus was taken up from us. For one of these must become a witness with us of his resurrection."

²³ So they nominated two men: Joseph called Barsabbas (also known as Justus) and Matthias. ²⁴ Then they prayed, "Lord, you know everyone's heart. Show us which of these two you have chosen ²⁵ to take over this apostolic ministry, which Judas left to go where he belongs." ²⁶ Then they cast lots, and the lot fell to Matthias; so he was added to the eleven apostles.

Acts 1 v 12-26

The previous month and a half must have seemed like an emotional rollercoaster to Jesus' followers. So much had happened: Judas, one of the twelve disciples, had betrayed Jesus (bad). Jesus had been tortured, tried, and crucified (unimaginably terrible). A couple of days later Jesus rose from the dead (amazing) and spent forty days with his followers explaining the Scriptures (wonderful). Then he ascended into heaven (thrilling but also a little sad) with a promise to send his Holy Spirit (exciting in a "what exactly does that mean?" kind of way).

Given all of that, it might have been a bit of a relief to be told by Jesus simply to wait in Jerusalem. We know from the Jewish calendar that there would have been about ten days between Jesus' ascension into heaven and the Spirit coming at Pentecost. And so in this passage Luke gives us a glimpse into what they were doing as they waited. It's a section of Acts that often gets skated over, sandwiched as it is between more famous action-packed passages. But Luke included it for a reason, and it's this: what we see in the life of these first believers is that the good and sovereign plan of God had worked everything out for them—and us.

A Sovereign Plan

At first, two men stand at the center of the action: Peter and Judas. Somewhat surprisingly, given his recent denial of Christ, Peter is the disciple standing before the assembly of believers, helping them make sense of what has happened and what still needs to be done. And the first thing that Peter does is address the issue of Judas, the proverbial "elephant in the room." Judas had been just like the other eleven disciples. He had seen, spoken with, listened to and gone on mission for Jesus. Then he had sold him. How could Judas have then betrayed Jesus in that way?

And so to address their concerns, Peter stresses the fact that God was in control of Judas' actions all along. The sovereign, unshakable rule of God stood over even the wickedness and cowardice of Judas. Judas' betrayal was not a surprise to the Lord. In verse 20, Peter says that the psalmist spoke about Judas centuries before he even existed.

Quoting from Psalm 69 ("may his place be deserted") and Psalm 109 ("may another take his place of leadership"), Peter sees the shadow of Judas in the words of King David. When David cried out in the psalms against the one who had dealt with him treacherously, he was pointing forward to Jesus, the greater King of Israel, who would be betrayed and persecuted by Judas. All of which is to say: this was God's plan. "The Holy Spirit spoke long ago … concerning Judas" (Acts 1 v 16). His treachery was not an accident; it was not a detour on the plan. It was part of it. Judas acted under his own compulsion, but not outside of God's will.

This point was extremely important for the fledgling church to grasp. At that moment, without Jesus, without the Spirit, few in number, surrounded by enemies and unsure of who in their midst might be another Judas, you can see why everything might seem to be hanging by a thread. How were they going to survive, let alone take the message about Jesus into the whole world? What they needed to understand most was that God was in control, even in apparent defeat or disaster. Nothing that had happened had frustrated his plans; all that had happened had furthered them.

We've seen that our job and our privilege as Christians is to glorify God by spreading his gospel truth in our lives, in our neighborhoods, to the ends of the earth. And if we are really going to do that (and not just pay lip service to the idea of it), we will need a firm grasp of the fact that God is in complete control of everything we attempt to do, and every reaction to our attempts. God does not need us or depend on us to accomplish his will; he simply gives us the privilege of being part of how he accomplishes it.

There will be times when it will seem that everything has gone off the rails: churches sometimes split, some ministers disappoint us, and some of the best-conceived mission programs bear little fruit. Oftentimes things move slowly in the realm of evangelism; sometimes decades go by without family members showing any discernible sign of interest in the gospel message. There will be times when people we love and trust turn out to be Judases. And at those times, we need to have Peter's speech here in the back of our minds, and say to ourselves: *God's good plan has this covered.* What looks like a disaster to me has not taken him by surprise or derailed his intentions. If Judas' betrayal could be used by the Father to take his Son to the place where he would win salvation for humanity, then any other setback can be met with the firm knowledge that God is working in and through it.

A Just Plan

In verse 18, Luke interrupts Peter's talk to tell us what happened to Judas. The ending of his life takes place "off camera;" we don't get a live report. Instead, Luke tells us that Judas bought a field and died gruesomely, his intestines spilling out everywhere. Judas' life did not end well. Wickedness quite literally bought him a grave.

Some people have perceived a difference between this account and the one that Matthew gives in his Gospel account (Matthew 27 v 1-10). This is not the place to get into addressing those concerns, but suffice it to say that both Matthew and Luke record the same things: Judas is overwhelmed with grief and guilt, he dies a gruesome death, a field is purchased with the money he received, and that place is called *Akeldama*, the "Field of Blood."

Why is it important for us to know what happened to Judas? Again, it is a reminder for us that God's good plan has everything covered. Judas' wickedness did not go unnoticed or unaddressed; he was held accountable for his world-class treachery. In the same way that the Psalms prophesied Judas' act of betrayal, they also predicted the curse that would come upon him as a result. In verse 20, Peter quotes from Psalm 69 ("may his place be deserted; let there be no one to dwell in it") to demonstrate that point. Judas didn't get away with it.

It is important to remember that Judas' biggest problem was not the explosion of his intestines (though, in fairness, that was pretty bad). What Judas really needed to worry about was facing God and being damned for eternity. We're reminded of this in the prayer that followed Peter's talk: "Judas left to go where he belongs" (Acts 1 v 25). They're not talking about a field in Jerusalem; they're talking about justice beyond death.

After all, if the only price Judas paid for his crimes was a nasty death, how would that be just? He didn't even suffer a fraction of the pain that Jesus endured because of his betrayal! No, final justice for Judas (and everyone else, for that matter) didn't come in this life. The nasty circumstances of his death were merely a shadow of the ultimate destruction for which Judas was headed. He did not escape justice.

And here's why Christians don't shrink away from the reality of God's judgment. It's good news that God's plan includes justice; that crime does not pay, but is punished. We all want a man like Josef Stalin, who died in his bed after sending millions to their deaths in the gulag camps (not to mention the forced starvation, show trials, and so on), to be brought to justice. Because there is a judgment, and there is a hell, he will be. We all want someone who abuses vulnerable people and gets away with it for his whole life to be unmasked. Because there is a judgment, and there is a hell, he will be. God's good plan has justice for all covered.

These days, "sophisticated" people do not normally believe in the idea of an eternal punishment in the afterlife. But that leaves them with a God who is indifferent to suffering, or who is powerless to punish it; or a world without a God at all, where what we call injustice is simply a rearrangement of atoms in a cold, impersonal universe. Praise God that he punishes sin in eternity!

Of course if we are honest, we have to admit that we deserve God's justice, just as Judas did. Our crimes may not be as flagrant, but our rebellions (large and small) against God are no less wicked. All sin is treachery against the King, whether by a kiss in a garden or by a lustful glance, a malicious thought or an angry word. And so the reality of God's justice is only good news for us because God's sovereign plan included Jesus coming to bear the wrath that we deserved on the cross. We have been spared from the punishment that we deserve by the sacrifice of Christ.

This changes how we look at injustice in our own lives. As Christians, we can be patient. We do not need to see justice accomplished in this life; we do not need to strive to settle every account; we don't need to work to ensure that someone who has wronged us or our loved ones to receive their comeuppance. God's good plan has it covered. "Leave room for God's wrath," Paul writes. "'It is mine to avenge; I will repay,' says the Lord" (Romans 12 v 19). God will punish those sins; either (like yours) at the cross, or in hell. And so you can forgive the wrongdoer. You can bless them and pray for them.

How the Plan Works Out

Peter understands that the Old Testament not only predicted that Judas would betray Jesus and face judgment for it, but that "another [must] take his place of leadership" (Acts 1 v 20). A replacement for Judas must be appointed.

It is not immediately obviously why there needed to be another apostle (beyond the fact that the Psalm Peter quoted seems to say so), but it may well have to do with keeping a certain symmetry with the Old Testament people of God. In the Old Testament, the people of God were organized into twelve tribes, so the leadership of twelve apostles seems to mirror that, reflecting the fact that this community of believers is the new people of God.

But what Peter does underline is the qualifications necessary for the new apostle. It must be someone who has "been with us the whole time the Lord Jesus was living out among us, beginning form John's baptism to the time when Jesus was taken up from us." Why? Because of the fundamental job of the apostles, which was to witness to the Lord's resurrection (v 22). After the believers prayed, they cast a lot—it fell to Matthias and he was appointed to be one of the twelve.

This little incident might seem like an insignificant footnote in a much more exciting, larger story. But it does show us something very important about the way that the Holy Spirit was going to work in his church. Remember where we are in the bigger picture: Jesus has ascended into heaven, and in a couple of days the Holy Spirit of God is going to descend on the church and things are going to get very exciting very quickly. There will be miracles, supernatural gifts, and displays of God's power going off everywhere.

But none of that is meant to supersede or replace the eyewitness testimony of the apostles to the life, baptism, teaching, death, resurrection, and ascension of the Lord Jesus Christ. The Holy Spirit wasn't going to come and teach or show or empower or do anything that contradicted or replaced that apostolic testimony. Instead, the Spirit would work through men who had a real and living experience of that real, human, historical Jesus.

This is a truth that Christians today often miss. The Holy Spirit will never say or do or inspire *anything* (ever!) that contradicts or undermines the apostolic testimony, found in the Bible, to the real, flesh-and-blood, crucified Jesus. The Spirit himself inspired that testimony, so how could he later contradict it?

Sometimes Christians pit these things against each other, as if we should expect the power of the Holy Spirit to come into our lives and bring some fresh, new, direct experience of God. But in fact, the Spirit loves to exalt and make much of the historical God-man Jesus Christ (John 16 v 14). And so he will never do an end-run around that revelation and reveal something different to us. We can identify the work of the Spirit in our lives as the word of God takes root in our hearts, received in faith and bearing good fruit.

To be blunt, people say all kinds of crazy things and blame them on the Holy Spirit. I have had different people tell me that the Spirit of God told them to leave their spouse for someone else, to stop reading the Bible, to stop going to church, and to not eat food on Tuesdays (no, no, no, and probably not). The Holy Spirit will never reveal anything to you or impress upon you anything that doesn't agree with the words and deeds of the historical Jesus and the testimony of the apostles (1 John 4 v 2). The promise of the Holy Spirit at Pentecost did not do away with the need for apostles to teach the gospel. God's sovereign plan was to have twelve men who would witness, in the power of the Spirit, to the truth that the Lord Jesus was born, lived, died, rose and returned to heaven to rule.

So if you want a powerful experience of the Spirit, if you want his guidance and conviction and comfort, you must devote yourself to prayer in the way that the early church did, and live with a keen expectation that the Spirit will be at work. But you must also devote yourself to the word of God, to knowing the real, historical Jesus through the Scriptures. Jesus is the One whom the Spirit comes to glorify. A growing love for Jesus and a character that is growing to be more like him is the experience of the Spirit.

How to Know if You "Get" God's Sovereign Plan

Here is how you can know that you have really understood the message about God's sovereign plan: you will pray. Sandwiched between two amazing statements about

God's mighty plan—Jesus' words about the certain spread of the gospel to the entire world in verse 8 and Peter's statement about the necessity of Judas' betrayal in verse 16—is this simple fact about the disciples and the other first Christians: "they all joined together constantly in prayer" (v 14). That is a pretty emphatic statement: they *all* joined together *constantly* in prayer.

The same dynamic is at work in verse 24. The disciples are choosing a new apostle, and they acknowledge in their prayer that the Lord is in control. They know that he knows everyone's heart, and so they merely ask him to reveal his choice to them. God's rule and control drives believers to prayer.

Isn't that amazing? You might think that the instinct would be just the opposite: God's got it under control, so let's relax. Why bother praying, since God has already decided what he's going to do?

But that's not how the disciples respond. They know God has a good, sovereign plan; and so they pray! They devote themselves to asking God to do what he has already said he is going to do; that is the logic of prayer.

The Bible holds two truths in tension. First, God is sovereign; he does whatever he wishes to do. In Isaiah 46 v 10-11, the LORD says:

> I make known the end from the beginning, from ancient times, what is still to come. I say, "My purpose will stand, and I will do all that I please." From the east I summon a bird of prey; from a far-off land, a man to fulfill my purpose. What I have said, that I will bring about; what I have planned, that I will do.

It is hard to imagine how God could be clearer: he knows everything and does whatever he wants to do.

But the second truth is the fact that God does respond to prayer. Jesus said:

Ask and it will be given to you; seek and you will find; knock and the door will be opened to you. For everyone who asks receives; the one who seeks finds; and to the one who knocks, the door will be opened.

(Luke 11 v 9-10)

When we ask, God opens up doors for us. Because he is sovereign, God *can* open up doors for us. When we are too lazy or indifferent to pray, God normally holds off his blessing until we acknowledge our need for him through prayer. In his wisdom and kindness, God has decided that prayer will be a means by which he accomplishes his eternal purposes.

God has declared that certain things are going to happen; this is his sovereignty at work. He has also decided that these things are going to come to pass through the means that he has decided upon—that is where we come in. God has decided that he will use his people's prayers and his people's lives to accomplish his will. God does not rely on our prayers, so that if I forget to pray for someone, they won't come to faith. But God does use our prayers, so that when I pray and see him answer, I can feel the joy of the privilege of being part of God's work in the world.

And so the mission of the church and the power of God should drive Christians to persistent, united prayer. Our prayer shows our humble dependence on him (he's the one with the sovereign plan, not me). Our prayer shows our great confidence in him (he's the one with the sovereign plan...) When we face what seems like a disaster... When we see flagrant injustice... When we consider the magnitude of the task of sharing the gospel worldwide... we remember that God is in charge, that his good plan has all of this covered—and we pray.

For Reflection:

- ○ *Are there areas of your life where you need to wrestle through the truth that what you are facing is part of God's good, sovereign plan?*

- ○ *Are there ways in which you are assuming the role of justice-bringer, in seeking revenge or witholding forgiveness? What would change if you remembered that God is judge, and is just?*

- ○ *What does your prayer life suggest about your appreciation of God's sovereign plan? What might change?*

When peace, like a river, attendeth my way,
When sorrows like sea billows roll;
Whatever my lot, thou hast taught me to say,
It is well, it is well with my soul.

Though Satan should buffet, though trials should come,
Let this blest assurance control,
That Christ hath regarded my helpless estate,
And hath shed his own blood for my soul.

My sin—oh, the bliss of this glorious thought!—
My sin, not in part but the whole,
Is nailed to the cross, and I bear it no more,
Praise the Lord, praise the Lord, O my soul!

For me, be it Christ, be it Christ hence to live:
If Jordan above me shall roll,
No pang shall be mine, for in death as in life
Thou wilt whisper thy peace to my soul.

But, Lord, 'tis for thee, for thy coming we wait,
The sky, not the grave, is our goal;
Oh, trump of the angel! Oh, voice of the Lord!
Blessed hope, blessed rest of my soul!

And Lord, haste the day when the faith shall be sight,
The clouds be rolled back as a scroll;
The trump shall resound, and the Lord shall descend,
Even so, it is well with my soul.

"It Is Well With My Soul" by Horatio G. Spafford

CHAPTER SEVEN

LIKE TONGUES
OF FIRE

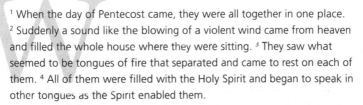

¹ When the day of Pentecost came, they were all together in one place.
² Suddenly a sound like the blowing of a violent wind came from heaven and filled the whole house where they were sitting. ³ They saw what seemed to be tongues of fire that separated and came to rest on each of them. ⁴ All of them were filled with the Holy Spirit and began to speak in other tongues as the Spirit enabled them.

⁵ Now there were staying in Jerusalem God-fearing Jews from every nation under heaven. ⁶ When they heard this sound, a crowd came together in bewilderment, because each one heard their own language being spoken. ⁷ Utterly amazed, they asked: "Aren't all these who are speaking Galileans? ⁸ Then how is it that each of us hears them in our native language? ⁹ Parthians, Medes and Elamites; residents of Mesopotamia, Judea and Cappadocia, Pontus and Asia, ¹⁰ Phrygia and Pamphylia, Egypt and the parts of Libya near Cyrene; visitors from Rome ¹¹ (both Jews and converts to Judaism); Cretans and Arabs—we hear them declaring the wonders of God in our own tongues!" ¹² Amazed and perplexed, they asked one another, "What does this mean?"

¹³ Some, however, made fun of them and said, "They have had too much wine."

Acts 2 v 1-13

Jennifer hadn't shown up for one of our church's meetings for a while. About a year earlier, she had accepted a friend's invitation to come along on a Sunday morning. Before long, the good news of Jesus' death and resurrection had changed her life. She repented of her sins and put her trust in Christ; not long afterwards she was baptized and became a member of our church. But after months of eager involvement, she had stopped attending altogether.

When I called her to find out what was going on, she was reluctant to speak frankly. After a number of evasive answers ("I've been a little sick... I've been traveling..."), she finally told me the truth. In her words, she wanted to find a church that "has the Holy Spirit." When I asked her what that meant, she explained she was looking for a church that was more exciting, that had more dancing and shouting, that was, basically, more "Spirit-filled."

I have to admit, that stung a little bit. No one likes to be told that they lead a church that seems to lack the presence of the Holy Spirit. But I know what she meant; in her home country, most of the churches spoke in tongues and had more exuberant forms of worship. Our congregation tends to be more contemplative and at times even somber—put it this way, not many people bring their tambourines to our church.

I talked to Jennifer for a while about her concerns; in the end, she chose to move on to another church. That didn't bother me in itself—as a pastor, I just want people to be plugged into a congregation where they will grow in Christ. I don't mind if it's not the one that I serve. But the conversation did make me think: what should people expect from a church that is "Spirit-filled"? What does the extraordinary ministry of the Holy Spirit look like in a local, ordinary church?

Maybe you have been in Jennifer's shoes. Maybe you've left one church for another because it seemed to lack, well, something of the Spirit of Pentecost. Maybe you've never left, but you have a nagging feeling that you're missing out when you hear about other churches and what happens there. Or perhaps you're moving in the opposite direction; you're from a church that does all that Jennifer wanted her church to do, and yet you still feel something's not quite right.

Pentecost—the day the Spirit came, as promised—is one of the most wonderful days in history. It's one of the climactic moments of the Bible. And it's also one of the most bickered about in today's church. Let's look at it now!

The Spirit of Jesus Comes

As Acts 2 begins, it has been about fifty days since Jesus was crucified, and ten days since he ascended bodily into heaven. When our story begins, the 120 disciples are all together in one place, probably the "upper room" in Jerusalem that Luke mentions in 1 v 13, and the feast of Pentecost has begun. When we hear the word "Pentecost" today, Christians think about these events that Luke records for us here in the book of Acts. But even before that, Pentecost was a significant time of celebration in the life of Israel. Moses had given instructions to the people of Israel (Leviticus 23 v 15-21) that they should gather at this time of year to celebrate Pentecost (also called "the Festival of New Grain" or "the Festival of Weeks") by offering sacrifices from the first portion of their crops that had come in. This celebration was a way of thanking God for his provision in the harvest.

The word "Pentecost" literally means "the fiftieth part," and the feast was given this name because it was held fifty days after Passover. Pentecost was observed in the spring, a fairly pleasant time of year to travel, so Jerusalem would often have a crowd of pilgrims from all over the known world in town for the feast. It was a perfect time for God to unveil the next step in his great plan of redemption— for the disciples to start going to the ends of the earth at a time when some of those ends had come to them.

As the disciples were gathered together during the holiday weekend, Luke tells us that a sound from heaven suddenly interrupted whatever it was that they were doing. This sound was "like the blowing of a violent wind" and it filled the entire house where they were meeting. You can only imagine what it might have been like to be in that room, suddenly hearing the sound of gale-force winds but not feeling anything in the room move!

As if that surround-sound experience were not enough, the disciples got a high-definition visual experience as well. After the sound of the wind began, they saw what appeared to be tongues of fire in the room (honestly, I have no idea what a flaming tongue would look like, but there seems to be no harm in letting your imagination work on it for a while!) These tongue-like flames then became very personal, dividing up and resting on each believer. At this point all of the believers were filled with the Holy Spirit and began to speak in other tongues by the Spirit's power.

Apart from being impressive, there is also great significance to the Spirit revealing his presence through wind and through fire. There are several places in the Old Testament where we see the presence of God made tangible for people through these signs. Job (Job 38 v 1), and Ezekiel (Ezekiel 37 v 9) both had encounters with God where his presence was made known to them in part through a mighty wind. In the same way, fire is a significant symbol in the Old Testament: the Lord appeared to Moses in a burning bush (Exodus 3 v 2), he led the people of Israel in a pillar of fire (Exodus 13 v 21), and he came to Mount Sinai in terrifying flames (Exodus 19 v 18).

It is not hard to understand what these symbols are meant to indicate. A fierce wind is irrepressibly powerful; a tornado or hurricane dislodges and removes anything in its path. Fire consumes and purifies, burning away whatever is impure or worthless. And that is who God is: unimaginably powerful, and white-hot in purity. In every moment from the garden in Eden to this house in Jerusalem, God's presence has meant terrifying danger for sinful people. And yet now, to a people purified by Jesus' death, God comes near; the Spirit comes into his people; and those people live, are empowered, are blessed and are changed.

The Spirit of Jesus is Glorious

The way that Luke describes this event is a helpful reminder to us that the Spirit of God is far beyond our comprehension and control. The Spirit came "suddenly," not in response to anything the disciples had said or done. He is sovereign and free; there is no human initiative here that compels or encourages him to come. We do not sing, worship, or pray him into our presence, nor ourselves into his presence. Frankly, we make him out to be far smaller than he really is when we think like this.

He is also outside the realm of our experience and understanding. Luke cannot describe the coming of the Spirit directly, so he has to use similes and comparisons; it is "like the blowing of a mighty wind" and "what seemed to be tongues of fire." That is as close as we can get to an accurate description of what we're talking about here. You can sympathize with the crowd observing all of this out in the streets, bewildered (v 6), utterly amazed (v 7), and perplexed (v 12). This was unlike anything that anyone had ever seen!

The rest of the New Testament shows us the ministry of the Spirit in all its glory. He gives spiritual life to people (John 3 v 5-8); he grows the fruit of holiness in us (Galatians 5 v 22-23); he helps us to pray (Romans 8 v 26); he wrote Scripture through inspiring its writers (2 Peter 1 v 21); he convicts people of their sin and coming judgment (John 16 v 8); he guides us (John 16 v 13); he enables the preaching of the gospel (Acts 8 v 29); he gives us gifts for us to use to build up our church (1 Corinthians 12 v 7). But here, we don't see any of that. At this stage, what he does is give God's people the ability to speak in foreign languages. Why?

The Spirit of Jesus Unites

We live in a world of barriers. It seems that we are more isolated and less in touch with our communities than almost any other generation. The internet makes communicating with people around the world fairly easy, but it does little to encourage us to get to know our neighbors or co-workers. In America, community planning tends to give priority to open spaces and distance from neighbors. Our homes are our castles, little bastions of self-sufficiency that enable us to pull into our garage and shut the door without having to engage with anyone else.

While those things create significant distance between people, perhaps no obstacle is more difficult to overcome than a language barrier. I live in a neighborhood where many people do not speak English fluently, and since I am unable to speak any other language, it is really hard for me to have a relationship with them. We sometimes have a non-English-speaking family over for a meal, and invite some bilingual people to come as well and help facilitate communication. But that is about the best we can do; realistically, it is going to be hard for us to be close friends. We just can't communicate; the language barrier is a formidable challenge. So it is no surprise that the topic of language is addressed here at the beginning of the New Testament church. If the church was meant to be a multinational institution (unlike, say, ancient Israel), how would the gospel message spread across language barriers?

The answer to that question came at Pentecost. The coming of the Spirit with the sound of wind and the appearance of fire had two immediate effects on the disciples. First, they all were "filled with the Holy Spirit" (2 v 4). This is the fulfillment of what Jesus had told the disciples before he ascended into heaven: they would "be baptized with the Holy Spirit" (Acts 1 v 5). The second effect is that the disciples all "began to speak in other tongues" (2 v 4). By the Spirit's enabling power, all the disciples were now able to speak in languages that they did not know (otherwise, they would not have needed the help!), but that their hearers recognized as their own language (v 11). The language barrier was crumbling down!

This was a pragmatic gift. But it was far more than that—it was emblematic, too. To see why, you need to go back to the very beginning. When God created the world, it was perfect and beautiful. It teemed with life; everything flourished and all human beings spoke one language (Genesis 11 v 1). But after mankind rebelled against God, things began to get progressively worse, until we read about a time when a large group of humans came together for the purpose of rebelling against God. They said to themselves:

Come, let us build ourselves a city, with a tower that reaches to the heavens, so that we may make a name for ourselves. (Genesis 11 v 4)

In their unity, they felt able to build a society that not only rejected God, but that ignored him. This was the tower of Babel.

In his merciful response (he could have just wiped them out), God scattered them and confused their language, ensuring that they would not be able to communicate together and plot against him. For sinful humanity, communication is a tool for rebellion against God. And so part of the Lord's judgment against sin is to spread humanity out and to introduce multiple languages, so they cannot unite successfully against him. The history of the world since Babel shows God's plan succeeded. Unity has proved elusive ever since.

Now flash forward to the day of Pentecost. In Jerusalem that day were people from "every nation under heaven" (Acts 2 v 5—of course, Luke is speaking from his limited knowledge here). They spoke a multitude of languages. And in Jerusalem that day was the Holy Spirit (v 4), enabling God's people to speak all of those languages. Why? So that everyone could "hear them declaring the wonders of God in our own tongues!" (v 11).

Can you see the bigger picture now? That bigger picture answers the understandable question of the multilingual crowds: "What does this mean?" (v 12)! The gift of tongues at Pentecost is a sign that God is undoing the effects of mankind's sin in this new era of the Spirit! If Babel was God's judgment on human pride and rebellion, Pentecost is the beginning of restoration and reunification. In his kindness, God is making things right. At Babel, humanity used their common language in a suicidal attempt to steal God's glory. At Pentecost, God restores their ability to communicate with each other so that they can unite together to praise his mighty works. Scattering has become gathering; confusion has turned to understanding.

Where will this end? One day there will be:

... a great multitude that no one could count, from every nation, tribe, people and language, standing before the throne and before the Lamb. They were wearing white robes and were holding palm branches in their hands. And they cried out in a loud voice: "Salvation belongs to our God, who sits on the throne, and to the Lamb." (Revelation 7 v 9-10)

If you are a Christian, you will be in that multitude, surrounded by people of every language, culture and color. You will be together, praising the Lamb who made you and saved you.

And Pentecost is the start of the journey from a hopelessly divided, broken world to an utterly united, restored world. God's purpose at Pentecost is that by the power of the Holy Spirit, worship should come to him from every corner of the globe. Every tribe, tongue, and nation should unite together to acknowledge the greatness of God and his salvation in Christ.

That is what the coming of the Holy Spirit is all about. That is the point of Pentecost, and the point of the miraculous gift of these tongues. These Jews from all over the world could go back and begin to spread the message there in the language of their homeland.

Spirit Hunger

So, what's the takeaway for us? Well, we need to cherish the work of the Holy Spirit in our lives and in our midst. It's only by the power of the Spirit that we can worship God, understand his word, and love each other in the church. The permanent, irrevocable presence of the Spirit is one of the chief privileges we have as New Testament believers.

But having the Spirit's presence should also create a hunger in us. Pentecost was a one-time event, but the work of spreading worship of Christ all over the world was just beginning. It is appropriate that the Spirit should have come during the feast of Pentecost, when the Jewish people were celebrating the beginning of the harvest. The harvest that began on that day almost 2,000 years ago continues on until this day! A Spirit-filled church will be a witnessing church.

Because that is the case, we ought to pray. Pentecost represents the first in a long series of extraordinary movements of God's Spirit in salvation. There have been times in the history of the church that the ever-present Spirit has been poured out with particular power on the church for the purpose of mission.

Seeing the power of God's Spirit at Pentecost should create a longing in us for God to move in a similar way in our day, making us bold, wise and powerful as we take the gospel to our neighbors, co-workers and families. And if we have that desire, then we should pray tirelessly, asking God to roust his church and empower it for the work of taking the gospel out. We should pray to the Lord of the harvest for more workers and more fruit by the Spirit's power. As Jesus told his disciples:

> *If you then, though you are evil, know how to give good gifts to your children, how much more will your Father in heaven give the Holy Spirit to those who ask him!* (Luke 11 v 13)

A Spirit-filled church will be a praying church.

But here's a sad irony about Pentecost. The Spirit came to unite God's people and invite people of every place into that unity. And yet we so often bicker and fall out about that event and that Spirit. We wonder, and disagree about, whether our experience of the Spirit should be as dramatic as the believers in Acts had; about whether we need to be baptized in the Spirit (and if so, when and how that happens); about whether the primary sign of having the Spirit is speaking in tongues, as those first disciples did.

This is not the place for a fully developed discussion of these matters, but let me put my cards on the table for you. It seems clear to me that all believers are "baptized in the Spirit" when they come to Christ. In 1 Corinthians 12 v 13, Paul assumes that all Christians have received this baptism in the Spirit; he writes: "For we were all baptized by one Spirit so as to form one body." Notice that the emphasis in Paul's words is on unity in the church. The baptism of the Spirit is not a second experience of grace that creates a hierarchy in the congregation (these people have been baptized in the Spirit, these have not). Instead, baptism in the Spirit seems to be an experience of the power and ministry of the Holy Spirit that every believer should expect to receive when they come to Christ. After all, the Spirit came to bring unity.

In the same way, we need to be cautious when thinking about speaking in tongues. There is significant disagreement among believers about the meaning of this phenomenon, but there are some things that we can say with confidence. To begin with, the particular gift that the disciples were given here in Acts 2 was the ability to speak in languages that they did not previously know. And when they began to speak in foreign languages, they spoke of the mighty works of God (Acts 2 v 11): Jesus' death and resurrection and ascension, as we'll see in the next chapter. At all times they were under the control of the Spirit; they spoke "as the Spirit enabled them."

Now, much like with the concept of baptism in the Spirit, there is some controversy about whether or not speaking in tongues is something that we should expect to see when the Holy Spirit comes to believers in the present time. We do know that many of the believers in Corinth were said to speak in tongues (1 Corinthians 12 and 14), though it seems that this was a different experience from that of the believers at Pentecost, since people in that church couldn't understand those tongues without interpretation. But the New Testament does not teach that every believer should speak in tongues as evidence of the Spirit's power in their life. It is not considered a sign of unusual spiritual maturity or evidence that the Holy Spirit is present in a unique way in a believer. In fact, the church at Corinth seemed to have lots of people speaking in tongues, but a serious lack of unity and personal holiness! Instead, the emphasis in Scripture is on the diversity of spiritual gifts in the church, the danger of exalting one gift over another, and the sovereignty of the Holy Spirit to give those gifts as he sees fit (1 Corinthians 12).

So while Scripture does not require us to conclude that no Christian should or will ever speak in tongues today, neither does it teach that all Christians and churches should expect to have this gift.

Spirit-Filled?

Remember Jennifer, the woman who wanted to find a church that was "Spirit-filled"? Well, in the end, she may have been looking for the wrong evidence of the Spirit's presence. External signs are really no help in determining whether or not the Holy Spirit is present. Exuberant worship might be evidence of the Spirit, but then again, people from other religions worship their gods with ecstatic singing and dancing. Great singing that moves us to tears might be evidence of his word, but then again, people are just as moved at the gigs of their favorite bands. Instead, what we see in Scripture is that the Spirit of God unifies the church and empowers it for bearing compelling witness to the greatness of Christ.

So how do we determine whether our local churches are "Spirit-filled"? Well, ask yourself: are the knees in this place bowed in worship and prayer to Jesus? Are the people here loving each other sacrificially? Are ethnic barriers being broken down as different kinds of people are brought together in the body of Christ? If so, you can be sure the Spirit of Pentecost has taken up residence among you.

For Reflection:

- *How has this chapter encouraged or excited you about the presence and work of the Spirit?*

- *How can you pursue and celebrate Spirit-given unity?*

- *If you met someone like Jennifer, what would you say to her about finding a Spirit-filled church?*

Breathe on me, Breath of God,
Fill me with life anew,
That I may love what thou dost love,
And do what thou wouldst do.

Breathe on me, Breath of God,
Until my heart is pure,
Until with thee I will one will,
To do and to endure.

Breathe on me, Breath of God,
Till I am wholly thine,
Till all this earthly part of me
Glows with thy fire divine.

Breathe on me, Breath of God,
So shall I never die,
But live with thee the perfect life
Of thine eternity.

"Breathe On Me, Breath Of God" by Edwin Hatch

THE CLOCK IS TICKING

¹⁴ Then Peter stood up with the Eleven, raised his voice and addressed the crowd: "Fellow Jews and all of you who live in Jerusalem, let me explain this to you; listen carefully to what I say. ¹⁵ These people are not drunk, as you suppose. It's only nine in the morning! ¹⁶ No, this is what was spoken by the prophet Joel:

¹⁷ "'In the last days, God says,
   I will pour out my Spirit on all people.
Your sons and daughters will prophesy,
   your young men will see visions,
   your old men will dream dreams.
¹⁸ Even on my servants, both men and women,
   I will pour out my Spirit in those days,
   and they will prophesy.
¹⁹ I will show wonders in the heavens above
   and signs on the earth below,
   blood and fire and billows of smoke.
²⁰ The sun will be turned to darkness
   and the moon to blood
   before the coming of the great and glorious day of the Lord.
²¹ And everyone who calls
   on the name of the Lord will be saved.'"

Acts 2 v 14-21

There is something about a ticking clock that helps me to focus. If I have a firm deadline for a project, I tend to work more and more efficiently as the "zero hour" approaches. When I was in school, it might take me twenty hours to finish the first half of an assignment but I would be able to finish the second half in the day before it was due. My wife mistakes this gift of late-stage laser-like focus for procrastination, but I am convinced that it is a sure sign of genius.

After all, things get more focused as the end approaches. As a hotly contested sporting event approaches the final whistle, everything becomes more intense. An error that could be easily overcome at the beginning of the game might be disastrous at the end. The effort increases as the clock winds down; there is no sense in taking any energy and strength back with you into the locker room. At "crunch time," coaches call for their best plays; after all, what is the point of leaving good ideas on the clipboard? Runners find an extra burst of speed as the finish line comes into view.

The same thing is true in more important matters, too. Distracted parents might spend more time with a teenaged child as they prepare to leave the home. Many people who spend their entire lives without any thought for God will suddenly become religious when they receive a terminal diagnosis. We live differently when we know that the end is near.

And here is the thing: the end *is* near. We're in the final chapter of human history, and the last line could come at any time. That's what Peter wanted the crowd in Jerusalem to see, as they lived on the first page of that final chapter. As we'll see, it's both a thrill and a warning to know where we are in time.

A Promise Kept

To be honest, this is not an area where I have a lot of experience, but my guess is that if you have to begin a speech by assuring everyone that you are not drunk, it is not usually going to go well for you. But these were unusual circumstances, to say the least. Some people who had observed the extraordinary coming of the Holy Spirit, and the disciples speaking foreign languages, had come to the conclusion that the disciples must have had a little too much wine (Acts 2 v 13). Maybe if you and I had been there, we would have been tempted to come to the same conclusion. It's always easier to make fun of what you don't understand than admit your ignorance.

In any event, Peter jumps in and points out that it is only nine o'clock in the morning. The unusual behavior of these disciples has a far different explanation: a long-anticipated gift is being sent. A promise is being kept, and prophecy is being fulfilled.

Peter quotes from Joel 2 v 28-32, saying that the Lord had declared that he would pour out his Spirit on all people (literally "all flesh"). This was a promise of significant change that would happen to God's people at a future date. In the Old Testament period, God's Spirit was given to certain people on certain occasions to empower them for certain tasks. People like Othniel, Samson and Saul had the Spirit of God rush upon them (eg: 1 Samuel 10 v 10), and so received strength and courage for the work to which the Lord had called them. The average believer, however, did not have regular access to the supernatural empowering and guiding ministry of the Spirit.

But one day, that would change. The Lord had promised through Joel that one day his Spirit would be poured out on all of God's people, regardless of gender (both sons and daughters, men and women), age (young men and old men), or economic status (Joel's prophecy mentions slaves, and in Peter's sermon these people are now called "my servants" by God). The gift of the Holy Spirit was going to be given to everyone and anyone who called on the name of the Lord. Now, one morning in Jerusalem, half a millennium after God spoke through Joel, Peter stands up and says: *You've just seen the promise kept.*

In the big picture, this fulfillment of Joel's prophecy highlights for us the power of the Holy Spirit's ministry in the life of the church. When the Spirit falls, people are changed. Some receive visions and dreams, still others speak in tongues, and all are set off on a life-long trajectory of growth in holiness (Galatians 5 v 22-23). When the Spirit falls, timid disciples become bold witnesses to Jesus, people speak in languages they do not know, racist Jews are reconciled to Gentiles, and Gentiles become God's people.

This was a radical development. In those days, equality and tolerance were not widely embraced virtues. But here God's Spirit has come to all of God's people without respect to age, gender or title. In the New Testament church there are no "insiders" and "outsiders;" the Spirit indwells and enlivens everyone.

Realizing this will help us to keep our perspective clear as we think about our own local church. It is a good thing to respect and honor people in the church who labor faithfully and set a good example for the flock, but we should resist the temptation to establish different tiers in the congregation, as if some Christians are functioning on a higher spiritual plane than others. That simply isn't the case.

The gift of the Holy Spirit also reminds us that there is simply no place for pride and self-reliance in the Christian life. Pride reveals itself whenever we think that we can live as believers on mission without prayerful dependence on the Spirit. It's easy, if we're built this way in our character, to have a "can do" attitude to our life and witness. We go out and get on with mission in our own strength. But if we're so able, then why would God tell the disciples to wait? Why would he send his Spirit? We need to replace our self-reliant "can-do" outlook with a humble "Spirit-can-do" attitude.

But equally, our self-reliance shows if and when we think we are too small or insignificant to be useful in the work to which God has called us. We never need to have a "can't do" approach—thinking we need to leave it to someone better, more expert or more gifted. We mustn't stay home because of our own weaknesses. God has sent his Spirit to you. There is nothing he can't do! Beware thinking about the Spirit like an Old Testament Israelite; every New Testament believer has the power of the Spirit to resist sin, grow in grace, and spread the gospel.

The Beginning of the End

The coming of the Spirit does not just revolutionize the way we think about ourselves and our fellow Christians; it also transforms the way we think about time itself. Again, this is rooted in the words of the prophet Joel hundreds of years earlier. Joel repeatedly called on the people of Israel to repent of their sin and rebellion in light of the coming "day of the LORD" (eg: Joel 2 v 1-2), a technical term that the Old Testament prophets used to refer to a time in the future when God would come in judgment to destroy evil and save his people. But before that day comes, Joel says, the LORD will pour out his Spirit and there will be an opportunity for salvation for all who call upon the LORD (Joel 2 v 32). So there will be a period of time when the Spirit of

God is at work in his people and salvation is widely available, followed by a terrifying day of judgment.

So as Peter stands there in Jerusalem at Pentecost, he is proclaiming that we have entered into "the last days," the last period of human history. The coming of Christ, the cross, resurrection and ascension, and the outpouring of the Spirit mark the beginning of the end. A new epoch in human history has begun; we live in a time that is fundamentally different than the era of history that people lived in 2,100 years ago (1 Corinthians 10 v 11; Hebrews 1 v 1-2; James 5 v 3).

All of this shows us that something decisive and enormous has happened in the coming of the Messiah and the outpouring of his Spirit. Jesus brought the kingdom of God to the earth in a display of mercy and grace. He declared that the end had begun, that human suffering and toil under the curse of sin was being rolled back. As a sign, Jesus healed the sick and raised the dead and made the blind to see. When he died on the cross, he paid for the sins of his people and purchased our forgiveness. When he rose from the dead, ascended into heaven, and sent his Spirit to his people, Jesus inaugurated this new era of mercy and kindness. That's the amazing reality of Pentecost.

But there is another stage in these last days, something that hasn't happened yet: a coming day of judgment. According to Peter (quoting Joel), there will be wonders in heaven and signs on earth. These will be traumatic and catastrophic signs: blood, fire, vapor of smoke, the sun darkened and the moon turned bloody. But as devastating as that sounds, all of those signs are just the warm-up acts for the main event—the day of the Lord.

This means that the coming of salvation in the person of Jesus and the pouring out of his Spirit on all his people has, in a sense, started the clock ticking. We're in the last days. The only thing remaining is the return of Christ in great and glorious judgment. The next step in human history, the next gigantic move of God, will be judgment for the human race. The countdown has begun—we just don't know how much time is left on the clock.

The notion of judgment is not very popular in our day. We don't like judgment; we prefer mercy. We think that God should be a "good guy" and just turn a blind eye to our faults and peccadilloes. And if you and I were ever to get to create and rule over our own universe, I imagine that we'd be free to run it in any way we see fit. (For the record, I would not run a universe well. I cannot even replace the spark plugs in my car without eleven trips to the auto-parts store.) But in the real world, you and I need to come to grips with the God who actually is, not the God who you think should be. And in the Bible, God states plainly that one day everyone will stand before him to be judged for what they have done. Jesus put it this way:

> When the Son of Man comes in his glory, and all the angels with him, he will sit on his glorious throne. All the nations will be gathered before him, and he will separate the people one from another. (Matthew 25 v 31-32)

As surely as the first part of Joel's prophecy was fulfilled at Pentecost, so the rest of it will be fulfilled on the coming day of the Lord.

So the most important matter for you to settle on this present day is how that future day will go for you. Our culture and our hearts encourage us to think we are basically OK people. Maybe you have that view. But that does not mean that God shares your lofty opinion of yourself. It is the judge's verdict that matters, not that of the person who is on trial. And God, as the coming of his Spirit reminds us, is a fire—a breathtakingly, life-takingly holy fire who burns up anything that is imperfect. *Anything.* Basically OK is not God's standard. Absolutely perfect is. He commands the people he has made to "be holy, because I am holy" (1 Peter 1 v 16). You and I do not, cannot, get to that standard. Nobody's perfect; and only perfect will do.

Blood, fire, and smoke are just vivid ways of describing a reality that we cannot begin to imagine. That is the point of Peter's words there in Acts 2 v 17-20: the end has begun. Judgment is drawing near. The promised next act in this cosmic drama is the day of the Lord, and as Peter has pointed out by his quote from Joel 2, God always does what he says he is going to do.

If you are not a follower of Jesus, this means that you are in great danger at the moment. The last page of this chapter of history may finish before you finish the last page of the last chapter in this book. Jesus may return today, or you may die in decades, in your sleep. I have no idea what the future holds for you or me, except that, one way or another, we will face God's judgment against our sins. And so Peter's words are warning you that you are in grave spiritual danger.

That's why Acts 2 v 21 is such good news. Anyone "who calls on the name of the Lord will be saved." You can go to Jesus right now for salvation from the day of the Lord. You can ask him to take the blood and fire and smoke that you face. And then you can know that the last chapter of this world is not the last chapter of your life. Why? Because God has not only "set a day when he will judge the world with justice" (Acts 17 v 31); he has also appointed the Judge—and he has announced his appointment by raising that man from the dead. The man God the Father will send to judge you at the end of the last days is the same man he sent at the beginning of the last days to offer salvation to you.

The resurrection shows us that judgment will come; the coming of the Spirit warns us that it will come next in God's great plan for his creation. We will all face Jesus. How much better to face him as your Savior and Friend than to face him as your Judge.

If you are already a follower of Jesus, the events of Pentecost should infuse your life with great urgency. We are living in the last days! But too often we are like children with homework that has no due date; we live with little motivation to action. Do we *really* believe that our friends and neighbors will face judgment on that last day? Do we *really* believe that just being nice is not enough to get them through when they face Jesus their Judge? If so, there is no time for complacency.

We are playing in extra time; who knows when the whistle will blow? We must live with extra focus, like an athlete trying to close out an important victory. Don't leave anything out on the field. The ticking clock should direct our time, our wealth, our everything. And, of course, the coming day of the Lord lends urgency to the task of global missions. All over your neighborhood, in your workplace or your school, there are people who will face the risen Jesus still in their sins unless they call out to him now. All over the world there are people dying still under the judgment of God. Love and compassion compel us to take the gospel message to them. The world is big, the need is acute, and the time is getting shorter every day.

The Spirit has come; it is a thrilling warning that the end will, too.

For Reflection:

O *How do you feel about the clock ticking?*

O *How will remembering the times we're living in affect your outlook or actions today?*

O *Do you tend to view God's judgment as a topic to be avoided, or as part of the gospel to be communicated?*

Facing a task unfinished, that drives us to our knees;
A need that, undiminished, rebukes our slothful ease;
We, who rejoice to know thee, renew before thy throne
The solemn pledge we owe thee to go and make thee
known.

Where other lords beside thee hold their unhindered sway,
Where forces that defied thee, defy thee still today;
With none to heed their crying, for life, and love, and
light,
Unnumbered souls are dying, and pass into the night.

We bear the torch that fluming, fell from the hands of
those
Who gave their lives proclaiming that Jesus died and rose;
Ours is the same commission, the same glad message
ours;
Fired by the same ambition, to thee we yield our powers.

O Father who sustained them, O Spirit who inspired;
Saviour, whose love constrained them to toil with zeal
untired;
From cowardice defend us, from lethargy awake!
Forth on thine errands send us to labour for thy sake

"Facing A Task Unfinished" by Frank Houghton
© *Overseas Missionary Fellowship*

CHAPTER NINE

BECAUSE DEATH COULD NOT HOLD HIM

[22] "Fellow Israelites, listen to this: Jesus of Nazareth was a man accredited by God to you by miracles, wonders and signs, which God did among you through him, as you yourselves know. [23] This man was handed over to you by God's deliberate plan and foreknowledge; and you, with the help of wicked men, put him to death by nailing him to the cross. [24] But God raised him from the dead, freeing him from the agony of death, because it was impossible for death to keep its hold on him. [25] David said about him:

"'I saw the Lord always before me.
   Because he is at my right hand,
   I will not be shaken.
[26] Therefore my heart is glad and my tongue rejoices;
   my body also will rest in hope,
[27] because you will not abandon me to the realm of the dead,
   you will not let your holy one see decay.
[28] You have made known to me the paths of life;
   you will fill me with joy in your presence.'

[29] "Fellow Israelites, I can tell you confidently that the patriarch David died and was buried, and his tomb is here to this day. [30] But he was a prophet and knew that God had promised him on oath that he would place one of his descendants on his throne.
[31] Seeing what was to come, he spoke of the resurrection of the Messiah, that he was not abandoned to the realm of the dead, nor did his body see decay. [32] God has raised this Jesus to life, and we are all witnesses of it. [33] Exalted to the right hand of God, he has received from the Father

the promised Holy Spirit and has poured out what you now see and hear.
³⁴ For David did not ascend to heaven, and yet he said,

"'The Lord said to my Lord:
  'Sit at my right hand
³⁵ until I make your enemies
  a footstool for your feet.'

³⁶ "Therefore let all Israel be assured of this: God has made this Jesus, whom you crucified, both Lord and Messiah."

³⁷ When the people heard this, they were cut to the heart and said to Peter and the other apostles, "Brothers, what shall we do?"

³⁸ Peter replied, "Repent and be baptised, every one of you, in the name of Jesus Christ for the forgiveness of your sins. And you will receive the gift of the Holy Spirit. ³⁹ The promise is for you and your children and for all who are far off—for all whom the Lord our God will call."

⁴⁰ With many other words he warned them; and he pleaded with them, "Save yourselves from this corrupt generation." ⁴¹ Those who accepted his message were baptised, and about three thousand were added to their number that day.

Acts 2 v 22-41

The concept of guilt is having a bad century. Sigmund Freud thought that most negative behavior patterns could be traced back to the guilt people felt in response to their impulses and actions. Subconsciously, according to Freud, all children fear losing their parents' love, and so guilt develops in a child to help them behave in a socially acceptable way, thus securing parental love and approval.

In fact, much of modern psychology has developed with the purpose of freeing people from these kinds of negative feelings. So while people continue to experience guilt, we tend to see it as something to be treated and done away with as soon as possible.

But as we continue to look at Peter's Pentecost sermon, we see a huge crowd of people who are suddenly overwhelmed by guilt over what they have done. And the Bible seems to indicate that their guilt is a good thing.

Remember, Peter is in the middle of his big message to the crowd in Jerusalem. He has just explained the coming of the Holy Spirit in light of the prophecy in Joel 2, and now he begins to explain to the crowd who Jesus was. Peter tells them that Jesus was a man "accredited by God to you" (Acts 2 v 22); that is to say, God had given them some key pieces of evidence that made sense of everything. It's as though, through historical events, God has hung an identification tag around Jesus' neck. In his sermon, Peter mentions four different ways in which God had borne witness to the identity of Jesus.

Miracles and Signs and Wonders

First, they could see who Jesus was by looking at the way God had worked through him in his public ministry (v 22). Jesus worked many miracles that demonstrated his power; he calmed the sea in the midst of a ferocious storm and cast out demons with a word. Peter also says that Jesus performed wonders. Jesus amazed people. He did things that left people stunned, confused and bewildered (eg: Mark 2 v 12). If you really know Jesus, he really amazes you.

Notice that Peter pushes his point home on his audience; Jesus did all of these things "as you yourselves know." Peter could assume that word about Jesus' powerful miracles and amazing wonders had made it all the way around Jerusalem. These were all facts that were not in dispute; there was no doubt that these things had happened.

The Planned Sacrifice

The second piece of evidence that points to Jesus' identity is his death. Peter doesn't pull his punches here. Jesus was handed over. And then, with the help of wicked men—the

Romans—his listeners killed him on a cross. "You ... put him to death" (v 23).

It is not immediately obvious how Jesus' death serves as God's way of giving accreditation to him. In fact, it seems like just the opposite. It seems more likely that the cross was God's judgment on Jesus, letting him be murdered like that.

But that's to miss the truth in the middle of Peter's account of what happened. Jesus was "handed over to you by God's deliberate plan and foreknowledge" (v 23). We've seen already that Judas handed Jesus over in one sense; yet in another deeper sense, it was God who did it. God the Father had sovereignly determined that Jesus should be crucified because he knew that only Jesus could bear the sins of his people. God the Son had willingly allowed himself to be handed over and put on trial and nailed to the cross. On the face of it, Jesus' death looks like proof that he was rejected by God. But when you look more closely, you see that it is evidence that he is the Redeemer sent from God.

Back From the Dead

The third piece of evidence that Peter brings to the table is the resurrection of Jesus. Peter says that though God determined that Jesus should die on the cross, he raised him up. In case you had any doubts, the resurrection is both a powerful vindication of Jesus' claims and the very destruction of death itself. Peter borrows a phrase from the world of childbirth—literally, he says that when God raised Jesus from the dead, he "loosed the pangs of death" (v 24). It's as if God has made death give birth, to do just the opposite of what it normally does. God has made the grave of Jesus a spring of life.

In a sense, Peter doesn't have to prove his claim. There's a tomb nearby that will either contain a body, or not. But nevertheless, he gives the two evidences that Luke gave to his readers. First, the Old Testament. In the Psalms, David had prophesied that the Messiah would be raised from the dead and never decay. That's what happened to Jesus, Peter says. And then second, eyewitness testimony. Speaking of himself and the other first followers of Jesus, Peter says: "We are all witnesses of the fact" (v 32, NIV84). At the heart of everything Christians build their lives on—at the heart of all that Christians stake their future on—is a fact; a cold, hard piece of history. *Jesus is risen* is not a vague hope, nor a spiritual feeling; it is something that happened.

And it is a fact that, when the Spirit works in people, changes everything. Here we have the first-hand testimony of Peter, a man who was once a faint-hearted coward, but now claims to have seen Jesus raised from the dead, and is boldly proclaiming that he is alive. And if you read the rest of the New Testament, you'll see that things do not really go all that well for the twelve disciples from this point on. They get beaten up a lot, thrown in jail some, and pretty much all die for their faith. They do not ride around in limos as the CEO of Jesus, Inc. They gain nothing from all of this if the resurrection is not true. No one would give their life for what they know is a hoax. The eyewitness testimony is compelling.

Exalted to the Right Hand

Fourth and finally, Jesus' identity is proven by his ascension (v 33-35). Jesus has been exalted to the right hand of God, the right hand being the place of power and authority. And again David is invoked as a prophetic witness. In Psalm 110,

David saw Yahweh ("the LORD") speaking to the Messiah (David calls him "my Lord"). David himself didn't ascend into the heavens, but instead he saw "his Lord" being enthroned on high in all power, with his enemies as a footstool.

Amazing works. Predicted death. Death-defying resurrection. And enthronement on high. That's Jesus' accreditation for his true identity. A great teacher only, a charlatan, a lunatic—none of these fit the facts. Who has God proven this Jesus to be? Peter's answer is there in verse 36: "Therefore let all Israel be assured of this: God has made this Jesus, whom you crucified, both Lord and Messiah." There's really no higher praise available. You don't get any identity greater than the Lord—God himself—and Messiah—the eternal, universally-ruling, infinitely powerful, promised King.

This is the thing that you must know for certain, and the reality with which you must come to terms: Jesus is both Lord and Messiah.

Jesus is Lord... and That's a Big Problem

Before you get too excited, though, there is a major difficulty with all of this. Jesus is the Lord and the Messiah (or, to use the Greek word, the Christ), the all-powerful One who reigns over his enemies, but Peter tells the crowd twice what they must have already realized in their hearts: they killed this Jesus (v 23, 36). Peter reminds them that a crowd in Jerusalem had cried out for Jesus' blood, they mocked and tortured him, and then nailed him to a cross to die under God's wrath. They had not just killed an innocent man; they had killed the innocent Christ. You really do not want the blood of the resurrected Lord of the universe on your hands. They could be assured that Jesus is Lord, but they could not be reassured by that truth.

Neither can we. Yes, you are reading this book thousands of years after these people killed Jesus. But remember—most of Peter's listeners were from out of town. Very few of them would have been in the crowd at Jesus' trial. They were not there. Neither were you. Yet still Peter says to them: "*You* did this." Why?

There is a sense in which every one of us is responsible for Jesus' death. If you are not a Christian, you have to realize that you are rejecting Jesus right now. You refuse to acknowledge who he is and you hate the claim of authority he makes on your life. So do not kid yourself: if you had been there in that place and on that day 2,000 years ago, and if you had really understood what Jesus meant when he claimed to be Lord and Christ, you would have been lining up in that crowd to get rid of him. You would have been howling for his blood and insisting that he die. Every time you sin, you make it clear that you reject Jesus' authority in your life and you add your voice to those in the crowd.

If you are a Christian, Jesus died for your sins on the cross. When the crowds taunted him and called for him to show his power by coming down from the cross, Jesus refused. This was not because he could not overcome the nails in his hands and feet, but because he would not leave the cross until our sin was paid for. Your sins and Jesus' determination to atone for them were what held Jesus there. This is why the sixteenth-century reformer Martin Luther used to remark that we all carry his nails in our pockets. You did this.

What Shall We Do?

So, how should we respond to these twin facts, that Jesus is Lord and we have all killed him? Let's allow the crowd in Jerusalem to be our guide.

When the people heard this, they were cut to the heart and said ...
"what shall we do?" (v 37)

They were "cut to the heart." As the Holy Spirit opened their eyes and their ears and their hearts, they realized what they had done. That truth lacerated them; they were devastated. If you really understand what Peter is saying here, you will be cut up at the deepest part of your soul.

So we need to ask the question of ourselves: *Am I?* Here is the challenge: Have you ever been cut to the heart by the depth and breadth of your sin? Have you ever felt heartbroken at what you have done? Have you ever wept at your sin, as Peter did (Luke 22 v 62)? If not, then perhaps you have not really come to grips with the fact that your sin is nothing less than a vote for the crucifixion of Jesus. When you hear of Jesus' suffering, you must realize that it was your sin that did that to him. He hung there because of you. It must cut you to the heart.

Here is how you can know if someone has been cut to the heart: they will ask the question the crowd asked. "What shall we do?" That's the question of someone who has finally realized what is going on. These people are willing to do anything; there are no holds barred and nothing held back. They just want to know what to do, whether there is any way out of the desperately dangerous situation they now find themselves in. They are willing for God to set the agenda through Peter and tell them how to be saved.

And Peter's response to their question is pointed: "Repent and be baptized, every one of you" (Acts 2 v 38). He is calling them to a whole-hearted turnaround. Up until this point, their lives had been lived in opposition to God and to his Christ. They clung tightly to their own control over their life. They did what they wanted to do, whatever seemed best for them. But now Peter is saying: *Let go of that. Turn from your rebellion against Christ and turn to him, being baptized as a public sign of your allegiance to him.*

This repentance that Peter mentions is more than just feeling badly for one's faults. It's not less than that, but it must be more than mere regret. After all, the crowd already had that. Instead, they needed to act on their regret and radically reorient their lives around Christ. There is no following after Jesus that doesn't involve a basic willingness to do what he says.

There's a Jesus who is very popular these days. We can call him Jesus-lite. He offers to do anything we want, without demanding anything in return. He allows us to pay lip service to him being King, while maintaining control of our lives. He's a fill-me-up-and-forgive-me-but-leave-me-as-I-am Jesus. The only drawback with Jesus-lite is that he doesn't exist, so he can't help and he can't save. The real Jesus is the Christ, ruling in power and glory. There is no coming to him without placing ourselves under him.

That's the lesson we have to take away from the end of Peter's speech. If you are not a follower of Christ, I pray that the Spirit of God would cut you to the heart, and show you who Jesus is and what you've done by living your life in rebellion against him. And I pray that you would understand the amazing grace offered to you by the one you have offended. Jesus is offering you forgiveness. He is willing to pour out his Spirit on you. He came to die for the sins of the very people who killed him. There is mercy for you; it is the free gift that God will give to anyone who turns from his sin and turns to Jesus in repentance and faith.

And for those of us who are already followers of Christ, the application to our lives is not much different. We experience the gift of God's salvation through repentance and faith. There is a one-time act of God there. But those things are also the continuing path of the Christian life. We never graduate beyond the need for repentance and trust; we never get past that point. In fact, the very first thesis that Martin Luther nailed to the door at Wittenburg in Germany when he aimed to begin a debate, and in fact began the Reformation, was: "Our Lord and Master Jesus Christ ... willed the entire life of believers to be one of repentance."

There is a definitive break with sin that happens when you are converted. But there is also a lifelong war with pockets of sin and rebellion in your life that continues on every day until Jesus returns and makes everything new. As a result, the Christian life is the process of being shown your sin by the Holy Spirit, hating it because it is opposed to the Christ who died for you, and then crying out to Jesus in repentance and trust. It is realizing that the same impulse that drove lawless men to reject Jesus and nail him to the cross still twitches in us. By God's grace it no longer defines us, but it is still there like a small pocket of enemy resistance in a conquered territory.

Perhaps if you were really honest, you would acknowledge that you are totally stuck right now. Maybe you are mired in long-term patterns of sin and brokenness, and things do not ever seem to change. If that is the case, then here is what's happening: you are holding on tight to the sins that you think are going to make you OK. You have fooled yourself into believing that if you want to be happy and safe and fulfilled, you need your sin. You feel that you absolutely need your anger, your lust, your greed and your unforgiveness and self-pity. So when you are upset, you stuff yourself with food to take the edge off. When you are lonely or bored, you find yourself gravitating toward explicit material on the internet. And in the moment, those things take the edge off. They soothe us temporarily.

And if you are being honest, you can't imagine what would happen if you really gave them up, because then you'd be out of control; you would have nothing to hold onto in those painful moments except Jesus, and you are just not sure that's enough. And so, even though in your saner moments you know that the sin you are holding onto is sucking the joy out of your life, sapping the spiritual life out of you, and perhaps killing your marriage or wrecking your relationships or stealing your time or health, you will not let go because deep down you feel you need it.

But the amazing news is that Jesus holds out his wounded hands to us. He has given you forgiveness and his Holy Spirit. He will cut you to the heart so that he can take away the cancers in your soul. Let his Spirit cut you now, so that you cry out to him. He is ruling. He is loving. He is what you need, and all you need. Whether for the first time, or for the thousandth time, or the first time in a long time, you can turn to him right now.

For Reflection:

○ *Meditate on the truth that you killed Jesus. How does that humble you and move you to praise him?*

○ *When were you last cut to the heart about your sin? What would it take for you to be affected in this way?*

○ *Is there a sin that you don't think you can give up? What are you looking for from that sin, and how will you find it in Christ's loving rule?*

Just as I am, without one plea,
But that thy blood was shed for me,
And that thou bidst me come to thee,
O Lamb of God, I come, I come.

Just as I am, and waiting not
To rid my soul of one dark blot,
To thee whose blood can cleanse each spot,
O Lamb of God, I come, I come.

Just as I am, poor, wretched, blind;
Sight, riches, healing of the mind,
Yea, all I need in thee to find,
O Lamb of God, I come, I come.

Just as I am, thou wilt receive,
Wilt welcome, pardon, cleanse, relieve;
Because thy promise I believe,
O Lamb of God, I come, I come.

"Just As I Am, Without One Plea" by Charlotte Eliott (Verses 1, 2, 4, 5)

CHAPTER TEN

DEVOTED

[42] They devoted themselves to the apostles' teaching and to fellowship, to the breaking of bread and to prayer. [43] Everyone was filled with awe at the many wonders and signs performed by the apostles. [44] All the believers were together and had everything in common. [45] They sold property and possessions to give to anyone who had need. [46] Every day they continued to meet together in the temple courts. They broke bread in their homes and ate together with glad and sincere hearts, [47] praising God and enjoying the favour of all the people. And the Lord added to their number daily those who were being saved.

Acts 2 v 42-47

Imagine being part of the crowd that day. You see the amazing signs, you hear the preacher's explanation, and you suddenly feel cut to the heart for your sins. Now you are ready to put your trust in Jesus and commit to following him; so you decide to be baptized. After standing in line with the other 3,000 new believers, it's your turn. You come out of the water, out into your new, forgiven, Spirit-filled life, and... now what?

Go to church.

Reading the book of Acts is a bit like watching a flower unfold. The cross and resurrection of Christ lead into his ascension and the gracious outpouring of the Holy Spirit on God's people. The end result, the fruit of God's amazing saving activity, is a group of believers who have been freed from their sins by the blood of Christ and brought together by the power of the Spirit. Going to church isn't an anticlimactic end to Acts 2, and to this book. It's a thrilling one, as we see what a community is created when the Spirit brings God's grace to bear on people's lives? At the end of Acts 2, Luke is clearly holding out the life of this first New Testament church as a model; it is a normative picture of what the church looks like under the direction of the Holy Spirit.

Of course, we should expect that there would be differences between our churches and theirs. A lot of time has passed and our culture is very different than theirs. It is natural that our language, dress and customs are very different from those of the first church. But we should also expect to see a basic continuity between that church and ours. We believe the same message that they did and we have the same Spirit, so we would do well to check if our lives and our churches have been formed along the same lines.

According to verse 42, as these 3,000 new believers lived together they devoted themselves to four things:

O The apostles' teaching

O Fellowship

O The breaking of bread

O Prayer (literally, "the prayers")

Nothing indicates that they had to be told to dedicate themselves to these things; it just seems to have been an expression of the Spirit's life in their midst. And so it is worth stopping to unpack these four ways in which the church lived in light of the Spirit's work, and to ask where we stand today in relationship to this standard.

The Apostles' Teaching

The word Luke uses which we translate as "devoted themselves" is literally "they were being devoted." It has the sense of a constant, repeated activity, so we could say that the first Christians were constantly devoting themselves to the teaching of the apostles. They gathered in the temple day by day (v 46), presumably in order to hear the teaching of the apostles. And so right off the bat we have a trajectory set for the Christian church: it is governed by the content of apostolic teaching.

Luke doesn't tell us right here exactly what "the apostles' teaching" was, but there is little doubt that they were teaching them about Jesus. After all, the apostles were uniquely qualified to teach on the subject. They had lived with Jesus; they had heard every word he had taught and seen all of his miracles. They had been there for those forty days after the resurrection when Jesus had taught them and explained things to them. What made their teaching different from any other was that it was authoritative teaching about Jesus.

So the Spirit-filled church was constantly devoted to the teaching of the apostles. Nowadays, we follow their pattern by devoting ourselves to the apostles' teaching, and the Scriptures on which they based their Christ-centered teaching on—the Bible; Old Testament and New. When we commit ourselves to the word of God, inspired by the Spirit of God, and communicated (largely) through the witness of the apostles, we are walking in the paths laid out for us by the first Christians.

If any church is to thrive and prosper, it must begin with a conscious commitment to submitting life, both together and as individuals, to the word of God. It is almost impossible to overestimate how important this is. If a church lacks the inclination or humility or patience or concentration to devote itself to God's word, there is really very little hope for it, because there is no way for believers to be corrected, and no way for us to be straightened out where we are warped, unless we will listen to God's word. The Holy Spirit inspired the word for our instruction and edification.

If we want to experience the power and presence of the Spirit, we should expect that it will often come through our giving attention to his word. If we want to be changed and built up, it will come as we listen and submit to the word of God.

But there is a danger here that we need to be aware of. It's possible to have a stated commitment to God's word but have a cold, lifeless faith. It is possible to say that you love doctrine (that's the literal translation of the word that Luke uses there) but be completely unchanged by it. And so there is a danger in learning to recognize good doctrine and applaud excellent sermons and think that we are OK just because we say we love God's word.

That's a recipe for dead orthodoxy, seen in churches where the gospel is preached but there is no power for changed lives, no joy, and nothing compelling for the world to see and know that Jesus is real. That was not the way of the early church; they were devoted to the apostles' doctrine and teaching and, as we're going to see, it affected the way they lived. They took the truth they were learning and brought their lives into alignment with it.

So there's more to this idea of devoting yourself to the apostles' teaching than just being in your church for the weekly sermon and taking notes. There is more to it than just reading your Bible at home. It is not less than that, but it cannot be only that. If we are going to devote ourselves to the apostles' teaching, it will mean listening to sermons and reading our Bibles at home with a conscious commitment to have the word point us to Christ, cause us to love him more, and dictate the way we live our lives in response to him. We will have to pray for the Holy Spirit to come in and use the word of God to mess with our lives, convict us of sin, show us our faults, and inspire us to be committed to change. In the end, it would be far better to have a short, poorly constructed, inarticulately delivered sermon that leaves you loving Jesus more and makes you more passionate about living for his glory, than to have an hour-long exegetical masterpiece that leaves you smug about how good your church's doctrine is.

Fellowship, Bread, and Prayer

Real devotion to the teaching of the apostles is lived out in daily and weekly practice. That's what this first church did. They were also devoted to the fellowship, breaking bread, and the prayers. In the New Testament, the word "fellowship" (the Greek word is *koinonia*) has the sense of sharing in something, having a common experience together, or giving someone a share in something. That same word appears in 2 Corinthians to describe financial gifts given to support other believers (2 Corinthians 8 v 1-4 and 9 v 13).

That seems clearly to be the case with the early church in Acts 2. They "had everything in common [*koina*]. They sold property and possessions to give to anyone who had need" (v 44-45). Now, to be clear, this isn't a sort of proto-Communism. There's no indication that there was a mandatory central pot where all goods were held and distributed. In fact, it is clear that Christians still owned private homes (we know this because the church met in them), and when two members, Ananias and Sapphira, got into trouble (Acts 5), the apostles made it clear that their sin was not in the fact that they gave only part of their money, but rather that they lied about it.

But what we do see here is a radical generosity among the church members. If someone had a need, it was met, so much so that in Acts 4 v 34 we discover that: "There was no needy person among them." It's important to realize that this impulse to share was not the result of signing up to a particular economic theory. It was clearly an expression of a deeper commonality that existed among these Christians. Because the Spirit came on the church, there was radical fellowship, where the needs of other people were more important than personal wealth.

But the fellowship of the church was not merely financial. These believers met day after day in the temple (v 46); and they met in each other's homes, breaking bread with glad and generous hearts and praising God together (v 46-47). What an amazing picture of the way in which the church related to each other! Presumably many of these people had been, until recently, complete strangers, but their shared faith had transformed them into a close family.

I am not suggesting that Christians must to do everything in exactly the same way that the early church did. For example, I would not say that we have to get together every day just because they did. In fact, it seems from other parts of the New Testament that the church fell into a regular pattern of specifically coming together on Sundays. But I would suggest that compared to them, most modern ideas of Christian fellowship are pretty tame. When we think "fellowship," we tend to think of a cup of coffee before or after church: short, superficial, and painless. That's such a pale shadow of what we see in Acts 2. It cost them the very things we hold most dear: money, time and privacy.

That is what is really striking about this picture; the intensity and the importance of the church in the lives of these believers. We tend to view church as a wholesome Christian activity for Sundays (and maybe a midweek evening, if you're keen). Christians should show up on most Sunday mornings, drop a check in the offering plate and chat with a few people. Duty done. Box checked.

That's hardly devotion, though. Devotion is a whole-life commitment. It accepts cost rather than cutting corners. It's worth asking which you feel yourself to have too little of: money, or time, or privacy? Now, what would it look like to have even less, so that you can give it to your church family? That's devotion to fellowship. While we hold back, categorizing church as an activity rather than a way of life, both we and our brothers and sisters are the poorer for it.

A People, Not Persons

So, how can we help our local churches look more like the early church that we read about in Acts 2? First, we have to realize that our salvation has a community aspect. This picture of the church in Acts 2 is showing us something important about what it means to be saved by Jesus Christ. This is the immediate fruit of Jesus' death, resurrection, ascension, the pouring out of his Spirit and the proclamation of his word: a group of people passionate for the Lord, *and* for each other.

Jesus saves his people into a community. In one sense, that community is the universal church, the fellowship of all believers in all places through all time. It stretches around the world and up to heaven. But in terms of the way you actually live out your life, that community is your local church. Jesus did not save you to be a Lone Ranger; he saved you to live as a church member and enjoy eternity in his city, *living with others.*

The church is where you begin to experience your future. If you think about the most prominent patterns of sin in your life (things like selfishness, anger, jealousy, greed, lust), these sins alienate you not only from God, but also from other people. They isolate us and exile us. So in the death and resurrection of his Son, and through the indwelling of his Spirit, God restores us not only to himself, but also to others. We have a common Brother. We have the same Spirit.

Of course, the Acts 2 church was not in heaven; it was not a perfect expression of the horizontal reconciliation between people that comes from the vertical reconciliation we enjoy with God. Your church is not in heaven, either; nor is mine. It is a church built on heavenly principles, but stuffed full of sinful people. That kind of community is not easy.

But that's kind of the point. Jesus doesn't take away all of the weirdness and angularity and social awkwardness and all of the personality differences. Instead, God uses those things to change us, to go after our selfishness and irritability and impatience. There's no way to live in fellowship with others that doesn't involve you growing in Christ and dying to yourself. Maybe that's why people seem reluctant to do it, but your involvement in the fellowship of a local church is an important expression of your salvation.

This is part of what a church is celebrating when its members take the Lord's Supper together, and perhaps this is part of what Luke is referring to when he says that the early Christians broke bread together. Communion is a sign of a local church's identity and common fellowship in Christ. The bread and cup remind believers of what Jesus did for them, and they take them together as a reminder that they are the result—a people who perhaps would not normally want anything to do with each other but who are now committed to fellowship together. If we are able to grasp how fundamental the church is to our salvation, we will be more likely to make it a priority like those first Christians did.

In the book of Acts, this transformed community was so extraordinary that it was compelling to the people around them; Luke tells us that they enjoyed the favor of all the people (v 47). And the fruit of this community was that many people came to Christ, as "the Lord added to their number daily." This is important for Christians today, because there should normally be no tension between the fellowship of the church and the church's love for the world outside. Instead, outsiders should be brought into contact with the extraordinary love of God's people and be struck with the reality of their faith. The church itself is meant to be a demonstration of the gospel; its very existence points to the power and reality of the gospel. It's seen in the way that, within the church, you love and serve those who are not like you; it's seen in the way that, outside the church, you love and serve those who don't like you.

The Spirit will normally work his mission out through churches that are being shaped by the word and living it out in community. In the words of one missions network, "the local church should be at the heart of missions and missions should be at the heart of the local church" (check out radstock.org).

Fearing the Lord

The second thing that we need to do in order to look more like that earliest church is to recover our fear of the Lord.

When we think of fear, we think of dread and anxiety in the face of something terrible. But in the Bible, fearing the Lord means living in light of his majesty and authority. It has the sense of awe and respect for God's power and holiness. You see that lived out by the early Christians (v 43)—they lived in awe of what God had done for them and was doing through them. The apostles were teaching with power and performing miracles that authenticated their message. And the church lived with a joyful, holy sense of awe. They knew that the God who had done this, who had sent Jesus and poured out the Holy Spirit, was no joke. He was not someone to be taken lightly and relegated to a peripheral role in life and relationships. He was not a bit player in the overall story. For these people, the Lord was an awesome reality.

But for many of us, God is comfortable. He is safe and quiet and doesn't want much of you. You don't have to worry about trifling with him; he's our co-pilot or our buddy. And there's a direct link between the way we live together and that mistaken view, that lack of awe at the reality of God. Because if you don't fear God, then you will accumulate wealth for yourself while your brothers and sisters are in need. If your soul is not in awe of God, then you will feel as if your time is your own and you will do whatever you want with it. If you do not fear the Lord, you won't devote yourself to prayer with God's people. You certainly won't risk telling people who don't know him that they need to be cut to the heart by their sin, repent and live with Christ as Savior and King.

There is no shortcut to being devoted. You can't just decide: "Hey, from today I'll be more devoted." Today will turn into tomorrow, into next Sunday, and devotion will never come. The way to foster devotion to church is to know, really know, God—to be in awe of his power, his majesty and his mercy.

Now, at this point it might be easy to see ways in which your church needs to change. If only the pastor preached better sermons, if only people were more loving and service-minded, *then* we'd have a church like the one in Acts 2! Naturally, we think of quite a few people who really could do with being a bit less half-hearted and a bit more devoted.

But the best place for change to begin is with the person who is reading this book. So if you have resisted getting deeply involved in a church because the people are lame or weird or messy, you are missing a beautiful opportunity to demonstrate the love of Christ by loving others despite their faults. And you are robbing others of a great opportunity to love you despite yours! If you expect perfection from everyone else in church, while holding back from giving your devotion to it, maybe it is time to stop demanding too much from others and expect some more of yourself.

If, on the other end of the spectrum, you feel burned out by all of the service you do for your church, remember that you have the privilege of playing a part in the much larger drama of salvation that is being acted out before the entire universe. There are no small roles in this company and no one in Jesus' service ever gives more to him than they get from him.

The book of Acts is a testimony to the power of the crucified, risen, and ascended Christ. When Jesus sends his Spirit, a people are created who reflect his character in their personal lives, their corporate worship, and their global witness. Even though we are separated from those events by thousands of years, we have the same Spirit and the same faith in that same Savior as those first Christians did. In that sense, the story that began at the empty tomb continues on today in our lives and in our churches, and will continue until the risen Jesus returns. It is the only story that will still be sung of as the risen Lamb's people surround his throne in a million years' time. It the story that you are part of, that the Lord Jesus has beckoned you into and is writing through you. Let it be the story that shapes all you are and everything you do.

For Reflection:

O *Do you tend to see yourself as a saved individual, as a member of a saved people? What difference does that view make?*

O *How has this chapter reshaped and challenged your devotion to and actions toward your church?*

O *How will you seek to make your life story part of the great resurrection story today, this week, and this year?*

Thy hand, O God, has guided
Thy flock, from age to age;
Their wondrous tale is written,
Full clear, on every page;
Thy people owned thy goodness,
And we their deeds record;
And both of this bear witness;
One church, one faith, one Lord.

Thy heralds brought glad tidings
To greatest as to least;
They bade men rise, and hasten
To share the great King's feast;
And this was all their teaching,
In every deed and word,
To all alike proclaiming
One church, one faith, one Lord.

And we, shall we be faithless?
Shall hearts fail, hands hang down?
Shall we evade the conflict,
And cast away our crown?
Not so: in God's deep counsels
Some better thing is stored;
We will maintain, unflinching,
One church, one faith, one Lord.

"Thy Hand, O God, Has Guided" by Edward H. Plumptre (Verses 1, 2, 5)

ACKNOWLEDGEMENTS

Like my previous book, *The Cross In Your Life* (or *Passion*, as it was originally titled), this book has grown out of a series of sermons preached to Sterling Park Baptist Church, Virginia. That congregation has been unfailingly encouraging and kind through my tenure as their pastor, and I have particularly felt the support of my fellow church elders in the past season. I am very grateful to God for the privilege of serving him alongside all the brothers and sisters of SPBC.

I am also grateful for the work and ministry of The Good Book Company. Brad Byrd, their US Director, has done faithful triple-duty as a good friend, co-elder, and sounding-board for all sorts of things authorial. I am very thankful for the editorial and alchemical work of Carl Laferton; on more than one occasion during the writing of this book he took a hot mess of a manuscript and charted a path towards something useful.

And finally, thanks are due to my family. With every passing year, I realize more about how much patience and kindness it takes to be married to me. That Karen has joyfully stuck with it for 17 years and shows no signs of flagging is a daily reminder of God's grace to me. I can't help but smile as I think about my kids, Kendall, Knox, Phineas, Ebenezer, and Harper. Without them my life would be significantly less fun. They provide the comic relief that makes life much more enjoyable; plus, their mom won't ride rollercoasters with me.

the**good**book
COMPANY

Opening up the Bible

At The Good Book Company, we are dedicated to helping Christians and local churches grow. We believe that God's growth process always starts with hearing clearly what he has said to us through his timeless word—the Bible.

Ever since we opened our doors in 1991, we have been striving to produce resources that honor God in the way the Bible is used. We have grown to become an international provider of user-friendly resources to the Christian community, with believers of all backgrounds and denominations using our Bible studies, books, evangelistic resources, DVD-based courses and training events.

We want to equip ordinary Christians to live for Christ day by day, and churches to grow in their knowledge of God, their love for one another, and the effectiveness of their outreach.

Call us for a discussion of your needs or visit one of our local websites for more information on the resources and services we provide.

North America: www.thegoodbook.com
UK & Europe: www.thegoodbook.co.uk
Australia: www.thegoodbook.com.au
New Zealand: www.thegoodbook.co.nz

North America: 866 244 2165
UK & Europe: 0333 123 0880
Australia: (02) 6100 4211
New Zealand (+64) 3 343 1990

www.christianityexplored.org

Our partner site is a great place for those exploring the Christian faith, with a clear explanation of the good news, powerful testimonies and answers to difficult questions.

One life. What's it all about?

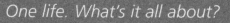